Prentice Hall ASE Test Preparation Series

Electrical/Electronic Systems (A6)

James D. Halderman, Professor
Sinclair Community College
Dayton, Ohio
ASE Certified Master Automobile Technician
ASE Certified Advanced Level (L1)
ASE Certified Undercar Specialist
ASE Certified Master Engine Machinist

Chase D. Mitchell, Jr.
Utah Valley State College
Orem, Utah
ASE Certified Master Automobile Technician
ASE Certified Advanced Level (L1)

PEARSON

Prentice Hall

Upper Saddle River, New Jersey
Columbus, Ohio

Editor in Chief: Stephen Helba
Executive Editor: Ed Francis
Production Editor: Christine M. Buckendahl
Design Coordinator: Diane Ernsberger
Cover Designer: Jeff Vanik
Production Manager: Brian Fox
Marketing Manager: Mark Marsden

This book was printed and bound by Courier Kendallville. The cover was printed by Phoenix Color Corp.

Pearson Education Ltd.
Pearson Education Australia Pty. Limited
Pearson Education Singapore Pte. Ltd.
Pearson Education North Asia Ltd.
Pearson Education Canada, Ltd.
Pearson Educación de Mexico, S.A. de C.V.
Pearson Education—Japan
Pearson Education Malaysia Pte. Ltd.
Pearson Education, *Upper Saddle River, New Jersey*

10 9 8 7 6 5 4 3 2 1
ISBN: 0-13-019187-6

Table of Contents

Preface

This study guide was written to help service technicians and students of automotive technology prepare to take the National ASE Certification Tests. This study guide includes the following features:

- **Sample ASE-type test questions** organized and correlated to the ASE test task list

- **Answers with detailed explanations** of why the right answer is correct as well as why the wrong answers are not correct

- **Heavily-illustrated questions and explanations** which explain the questions and answers.

- **A CD ROM** that includes additional study questions with answers plus additional study material to help the reader gain the knowledge necessary to successfully pass the ASE Certification Test

- **A coupon for FREE access to a Web site** for additional test questions that are graded online as you complete each 10-question quiz

- **A comprehensive English and Spanish language glossary** that gives detailed definitions of all technical words and terms used in the ASE Certification Test

- **Two appendixes** that address ASE assumed knowledge of environmental/ hazardous material handling and safety issues.

- **An index** allowing key words or topics to be quickly located.

About the ASE Tests

What is ASE?

ASE is an abbreviation for the **National Institute for Automotive Service Excellence** (simply known as ASE), which was formed in 1972 to provide standardized testing of service technicians.
ASE is a nonprofit association, and its main goal is to improve the quality of vehicle service through testing and volunteer certification.

What areas of vehicle service are covered by the ASE tests?

Automobile test service areas include:

A1 Engine Repair
A2 Automatic Transmission/Transaxle
A3 Manual Drive Train and Axles
A4 Suspension and Steering
A5 Brakes
A6 Electrical/Electronic Systems
A7 Heating and Air Conditioning
A8 Engine Performance

If a technician takes and passes all eight of the automobile tests and has achieved two or more years of work experience, ASE will award the designation of **ASE Certified Master Automobile Technician.** Contact ASE for other certification areas.

How can I contact ASE?

ASE
101 Blue Seal Drive, SE
Suite 101
Leesburg, VA 20175

Toll free: 1-877-ASE-TECH (273-8324)
　　　　　1-703-669-6600
Web site: www.asecert.org

When are the tests given and where?

The ASE tests are given at hundreds of test sites in early May and early November of each year. Deadline for registration is usually in late March for the May tests and in late September for the November tests. Consult the ASE registration booklet or Web site for details and locations of the test sites.

What do I have to do to register?

You can register for the ASE tests in three ways:

1. Mail in the registration form that is in the registration booklet.
2. Register online at www.asecert.org.
3. Telephone at (703) 669-6600

Call ASE toll-free at 1-877-273-8324 or visit the Web site for details about cost and dates.

How many years of work experience are needed?

ASE requires that you have two or more years of full-time, hands-on working experience either as an automobile, truck, truck equipment, or school bus technician, engine machinist, or in collision repair, refinishing, or damage analysis and estimating for certification, except as noted below. If you have *not* previously provided work experience information, you will receive a Work Experience Report Form with your admission ticket. You *must* complete and return this form to receive a certificate.

Substitutions for work experience. You may receive credit for up to one year of the two-year work experience requirement by substituting relevant formal training in one, or a combination, of the following:

High School Training: Three full years of training, either in automobile/truck/school bus repair or in collision repair, refinishing, or damage estimating, may be substituted for one year of work experience.

Post-High School Training: Two full years of post-high school training in a public or private trade school, technical institute, community or four-year college, or in an apprenticeship program may be counted as one year of work experience.

Short Courses: For shorter periods of post-high school training, you may substitute two months of training for one month of work experience.

You may receive full credit for the two-year work experience requirement with the following:

Completion of Apprenticeship: Satisfactory completion of either a three-or-four-year bona fide apprenticeship program.

Are there any hands-on activities on the ASE test?

No. All ASE tests are written using objective-type questions, meaning that you must select the correct answer from four possible alternatives.

Who writes the ASE questions?

All ASE test questions are written by a panel of industry experts, educators, and experienced ASE certified service technicians. Each question is reviewed by the committee and it is checked for the following:

- **Technically accurate.** All test questions use the correct terms and only test for vehicle manufacturer's recommended service procedures. Slang is not used nor are any aftermarket accessories included on the ASE test.

- **Manufacturer neutral.** All efforts are made to avoid using vehicle or procedures that are manufacturer specific such as to General Motors vehicles or to Toyotas. A service technician should feel comfortable about being able to answer the questions regardless of the type or brand of vehicle.

- **Logical answers.** All effort is made to be sure that all answers (not just the correct answers) are possible. While this may seem to make the test tricky, it is designed to test for real knowledge of the subject.

- **Random answer.** All efforts are made to be sure that the correct answers are not always the longest answer or that one letter, such as **c**, is not used more than any other letter.

What types of questions are asked on the ASE test?

All ASE test questions are objective. This means that there will not be questions where you will have to write an answer. Instead, all you have to do is select one of the four possible answers and place a mark in the correct place on the score sheet.

- **Multiple-choice questions**

This type of question has one correct (or mostly correct) answer (called the key) and three incorrect answers (called distracters). A multiple-choice question example:

What part of an automotive engine does not move?

    a. Piston
    b. Connecting rod
    c. Block
    d. Valve

The correct answer is **c** (block). This type of question asks for a specific answer. Answer **a** (piston), **b** (connecting rod), and **d** (valve) all move during normal engine operation. The best answer is **c** (block) because even though it may vibrate, it does not move as the other parts do.

4

- **Technician A and Technician B questions**

This type of question is generally considered to be the most difficult according to service technicians who take the ASE test. A situation or condition is usually stated and two technicians (A and B) say what they think could be the correct answer and you must decide which technician is correct.

    a. Technician A only
    b. Technician B only
    c. Both Technicians A and B
    d. Neither Technician A nor B

The best way to answer this type of question is to carefully read the question and consider Technician A and Technician B answers to be solutions to a true or false question. If Technician A is correct, mark on the test by Technician A the letter T for true. (Yes, you can write on the test.) If Technician B is also correct, write the letter T for true by Technician B. Then mark **c** on your test score sheet, for both technicians are correct.

    Example:

        Two technicians are discussing an engine that has lower than specified fuel pressure. Technician A says that the fuel pump could be the cause. Technician B says that the fuel pressure regulator could be the cause.

    Which technician is correct?

    a. Technician A only
    b. Technician B only
    c. Both Technicians A and B
    d. Neither Technician A nor B

Analysis:

> Is Technician A correct? The answer is yes because if the fuel pump was defective, the pump pressure could be lower than specified by the vehicle manufacturer. Is Technician B correct? The answer is yes because a stuck open or a regulator with a weak spring could be the cause of lower than specified fuel pressure. The correct answer is therefore **c** (Both Technicians A and B are correct).

- **Most-likely-type questions**

This type of question asks which of the four possible items listed is the most likely to cause the problem or symptom. This type of question is often considered to be difficult because recent experience may lead you to answer the question incorrectly because even though it is possible, it is not the "most likely."

Example:

> Which of the items below is the most likely to cause blue exhaust at engine start?
>
> **a. Valve stem seals**
> b. Piston rings
> c. Clogged PCV valve
> d. A stuck oil pump regulator valve

Analysis:

> The correct answer is **a** because valve stem seals are the most likely to cause this problem. Answer **b** is not correct because even though worn piston rings can cause the engine to burn oil and produce blue exhaust smoke, it is not the most likely cause of blue smoke at engine start. Answers **c** and **d** are not correct because even though these items could contribute to the engine burning oil and producing blue exhaust smoke, they are not the most likely.

- **Except-type questions**

ASE will sometimes use a question that includes answers that are all correct except one. You have to determine which of the four questions is not correct.

Example:

A radiator is being pressure tested using a hand-operated tester. This test will check for leaks in all except:

a. Radiator
b. Heater core
c. Water pump
d. Evaporator

Analysis:

The correct answer is **d** because the evaporator is not included in the cooling system and will not be pressurized during this test. Answers **a** (radiator), **b** (heater core), and **c** (water pump) are all being tested under pressure exerted on the cooling system by the pressure tester.

- **Least-likely-type questions**

Another type of question asked on many ASE tests is a question that asks which of the following is least likely to be the cause of a problem or symptom. In other words, all of the answers are possible, but it is up to the reader to determine which answer is the least likely to be correct.

Example:

Which of the following is the least likely cause of low oil pressure?

a. Clogged oil pump screen
b. Worn main bearing
c. Worn camshaft bearing
d. Worn oil pump

Analysis:

The correct answer is **c** because even though worn camshaft bearings can cause low oil pressure, the other answers are more likely to be the cause.

Should I guess if I don't know the answer?

Yes. ASE tests simply record the correct answers, and by guessing, you will have at least a 25% (1 out of 4) chance. If you leave the answer blank, it will be scored as being incorrect. Instead of guessing entirely, try to eliminate as many of the answers as possible as not being very likely. If you can eliminate two out of the four, you have increased your chance of guessing to 50% (two out of four).

HINT: Never change an answer. Some research has shown that your first answer is most likely to be correct. It is human nature to read too much into the question rather than accept the question as it was written.

Is each test the same every time I take it?

No. ASE writes many questions for each area and selects from this "test bank" for each test session. You may see some of the same questions if you take the same test in the spring and then again in the fall, but you will also see many different questions.

Can I write or draw on the test form?

Yes. You may write or figure on the test, but do not write on the answer form or it can be misread during scanning and affect your score. You turn in your test and the answer form at the end of the session and the test is not reused.

Can I skip questions I don't know and come back to answer later?

Yes. You may skip a question if you wish, but be sure to mark the question and return to answer the question later. It is often recommended to answer the question or guess and go on with the test so that you do not run out of time to go back over the questions.

How much time do I have to take the tests?

All ASE test sessions are 4 hours and 15 minutes long. This is usually enough time for you to take up to four certification tests. ASE recommends that you do not attempt to take more than 225 questions or four tests at any one session. The ASE tests are spread over four days so it is possible to take all eight ASE test areas during a test period (spring or fall).

Will I have to know specifications and gauge readings?

Yes and no. You will be asked the correct range for a particular component or operation and you must know about what the specification should be. Otherwise, the questions will state that the value is less than or greater than the allowable specification. The question will deal with how the service technician should proceed or what action should be taken.

Can I take a break during the test?

Yes, you may use the restroom after receiving permission from the proctor of the test site.

Can I leave early if I have completed the test(s)?

Yes, you may leave quietly after you have completed the test(s). You must return the score sheet(s) and the test booklets as you leave.

How are the tests scored?

The ASE tests are machine scored and the results tabulated by American College Testing (ACT).

What percentage do I need to achieve to pass the ASE test?

While there is no exact number of questions that must be answered correctly in each area, an analysis of the test results indicate that the percentage needed to pass varies from 61% to 69%. Therefore, in order to pass the Electrical/Electronic Systems (A6) ASE certification test, you will have to answer about 33 questions correct out of 50. In other words, you can miss about 17 questions and still pass.

What happens if I do not pass? Do I have to wait a year before trying again?

No. If you fail to achieve a passing score on any ASE test, you can take the test again at the next testing session (in May or November).

Do I have to pay another registration fee if I already paid it once?

Yes. The registration fee is due at every test session in May or November whether you select to take one or more ASE tests. Therefore, it is wise to take as many tests as you can at each test session.

How long do I have to wait to know the results?

You will receive written notice within two months after the test. Notification is sent out in July for the May test and in January for the November test sessions. You will be notified that you either "passed" a test(s) or that "more preparation is needed," meaning that you did not score high enough to pass the test and be rewarded with certification in the content area.

Will I receive notice of which questions I missed?

ASE sends out a summary of your test results, which shows how many questions you missed in each category, but not individual questions.

Will ASE send me the correct answers to the questions I missed so I will know how to answer them in the future?

No. ASE will not send you the answers to test questions.

Are the questions in this study guide actual ASE test questions?

No. The test questions on the actual ASE certification tests are copyrighted and cannot be used by others. The test questions in this study guide cover the same technical information and the question format is similar to the style used on the actual test.

Test Taking Tips

Start Now

Even if you have been working on vehicles for a long time, taking an ASE certification test can be difficult. The questions will not include how things work or other "textbook" knowledge. The questions are based on "real world" diagnosis and service. The tests may seem tricky to some because the "distracters" (the wrong answers) are designed to be similar to the correct answer.

If this is your first time taking the test or you are going to recertify, start now to prepare. Allocate time each day to study.

Practice Is Important

Many service technicians do not like taking tests. As a result, many technicians rush through the test to get the pain over with quickly. Also, many service technicians have lots of experiences on many different vehicles. This is what makes them good at what they do, but when an everyday problem is put into a question format (multiple choice), the answer may not be as clear as your experience has taught you.

Keys to Success

The key to successful test taking includes:

- Practice answering similar type questions.
- Carefully read each question two times to make sure you understand the question.
- Read each answer.
- Pick the best answer.
- Avoid reading too much into each question.
- Do not change an answer unless you are sure that the answer is definitely wrong.
- Look over the glossary of automotive terms for words that are not familiar to you.

The best preparation is practice, practice, and more practice. This is where using the ASE Test Prep practice tests can help.

Prepare Mentally

Practicing also helps relieve another potential problem many people have called "chronic test syndrome." This condition is basically an inability to concentrate or focus during a test. The slightest noise, fear of failure, and worries about other things all contribute. The best medicine is practice, practice, and more practice. With practice, test taking becomes almost second nature.

Prepare Physically

Be prepared physically. Get enough sleep and eat right.

One Month Before the Test

- Budget your time for studying. On average you will need 4 to 6 hours of study for each test that you are taking.
- Use the ASE Test Prep Online test preparation service three or more times a week for your practice.
- Study with a friend or a group if possible.

The Week Before the Test

- Studying should consist of about 2 hours of reviewing for each test being taken.
- Make sure you know how to get to the testing center. If possible drive to the test site and locate the room.
- Get plenty of rest.

The Day of the Test

- Study time is over.
- Keep your work schedule light or get the day off if possible.
- Eat a small light meal the evening of the test.
- Drink a large glass of water 1 to 2 hours before the test. (The brain and body work on electrical impulses, and water is used as a conductor.)
- Arrive at least 30 minutes early at the test center. Be ready to start on time.

What to Bring to the Test

- A photo ID.
- Your Entry Ticket that came with your ASE packet.
- Two sharpened #2 pencils.

During the Test

- BREATHE (oxygen is the most important nutrient for the brain.)
- Read every question TWICE.
- Read ALL the ANSWERS.
- If you have trouble with a question, leave it blank and continue. At the end of the test, go back and try any skipped questions. (Frequently, you will get a hint in another question that follows.)

Study Guide and ASE Test Correlation Chart

This ASE study guide is divided into the sub-content areas that correlate to the actual ASE certification test as follows:

Test Area Covered	Number of ASE Certification Test Questions	Number of Study Guide Questions
Electrical/Electronic Systems (A6)	**50 total**	**122 total**
A. General Electrical/ Electronic System Diagnosis	13	30 (# 1-#30*)
B. Battery Diagnosis and Service	4	14 (#31-#44)
C. Starting System Diagnosis and Repair	5	15 (#45-#59)
D. Charging System Diagnosis and Repair	5	12 (#60-#71)
E. Lighting Systems, Diagnosis and Repair	6	15 (#72-#86)
F. Gauges, Warning Devices, and Driver Info Systems Diagnosis and Repair	6	9 (#87-#95)
G. Horn and Wiper/Washer Diagnosis and Repair	3	11 (#96-#106)
H. Accessories Diagnosis and Repair	8	16 (#107-#122)

*The study guide questions are numbered consecutively to make it easier to locate the correct answers in the back of the book.

Electrical/Electronic Systems (A6)

A. General Electrical/Electronic System Diagnosis Questions

1. Technician A says a *short to voltage* may or may not blow a fuse and may or may not affect more than one circuit. Technician B says that a *short to ground* (grounded) will usually cause a decrease in circuit resistance and an increase in current flow. Which technician is correct?

   a. Technician A only
   b. Technician B only
   c. Both Technicians A and B
   d. Neither Technician A nor B

2. Why is it important to verify the reported electrical symptom?

   a. The problem may be intermittent
   b. There may be related symptoms not reported by the customer
   c. The service advisor may have misunderstood the problem
   d. All of the above are correct

3. A jumper is being used to bypass a switch to check the operation of the accessory lights as shown. Technician A says that the jumper wire should be fused for extra protection to avoid the possibility of doing harm to the circuit wiring. Technician B says that a jumper wire should not be used to bypass a switch during testing to prevent overheating the wires. Which technician is correct?

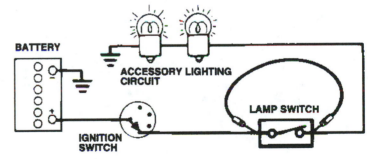

   a. Technician A only
   b. Technician B only
   c. Both Technicians A and B
   d. Neither Technician A nor B

4. How would you tell if a fusible link is blown?

   a. Cut the insulation open and inspect the wire
   b. Replace the fusible link and see if current flows
   c. Pull both ends to see if the link stretches
   d. Cut the link in the middle and make sure that both ends are intact

5. What is the first step in the troubleshooting procedure?

    a. Check hints and troubleshooting guidelines
    b. Diagnose the malfunction
    c. Perform a thorough visual inspection
    d. Verify the complaint (concern)

6. A fuse keeps blowing. Technician A says that a test light can be used in place of the fuse and unplug components in the circuit until the test light goes out. Technician B says that a circuit breaker can be used in the place of the fuse. Which technician is correct?

    a. Technician A only
    b. Technician B only
    c. Both Technician A and B
    d. Neither Technician A nor B

7. What is the meter measuring?

    a. Resistance (ohms)
    b. Current (amperes)
    c. Voltage drop
    d. Available voltage

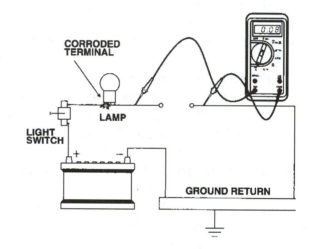

8. Technician A says that a low or zero reading on an ohmmeter indicates continuity. Technician B says that an ohmmeter set on the highest scale and reading infinity means no continuity. Which technician is correct?

    a. Technician A only
    b. Technician B only
    c. Both Technician A and B
    d. Neither Technician A nor B

9. A DMM set to read KΩ reads OL on the display. This means that the component or circuit being measured _____.

    a. Is open
    b. Is shorted
    c. Is OK – normal reading
    d. Has low resistance

10. If a digital meter face shows 0.93 when set to read K ohms, the reading means _____.

      a. 93 ohms
      b. 930 ohms
      c. 9300 ohms
      d. 93,000 ohms

11. A reading of 432 shows on the face of the meter set to the millivolt scale. The reading means _____.

      a. 0.432 volts
      b. 4.32 volts
      c. 43.2 volts
      d. 4320 volts

12. If a component such as a dome light has power (voltage) on both the power side and the ground side of the bulb, this indicates _____.

      a. A defective (open) bulb
      b. A short-to-ground
      c. A corroded bulb socket
      d. An open ground-side circuit

13. A circuit that has a relay does not work but the relay can be heard to click when activated. Technician A says the coil of the relay could be open. Technician B says that the coil of the relay could be shorted. Which technician is correct?

      a. Technician A only
      b. Technician B only
      c. Both Technicians A and B
      d. Neither Technician A nor B

14. The voltage is being checked at several locations as shown in the figure. Technician A says that the circuit is OK. Technician B says that there is a fault with lamps A and B because the voltage is lower after the current flows through the two lamps. Which technician is correct?

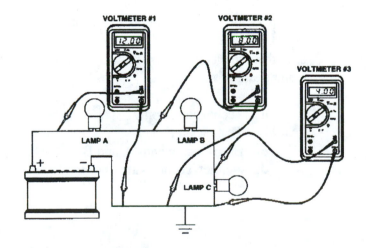

      a. Technician A only
      b. Technician B only
      c. Both Technicians A and B
      d. Neither Technician A nor B

15. The trunk release will not operate from the dash switch but will operate from the remote. Which is the *most likely* cause?

    a. A defective trunk release solenoid
    b. A poor ground at the trunk release solenoid
    c. A shorted dash switch
    d. The valet switch in the glove compartment is set to the lock position.

16. One fog light is out. The technician is checking to see if electrical power is available at the socket. Which position on the digital multimeter (DMM) should the technician select?

    a. DC V
    b. DC A
    c. Ω
    d. AC V

17. The motor circuit shown is being tested by measuring the voltage at several locations in the circuit. What is the *most likely* cause?

    a. Normal operation – no fault
    b. High resistance in the motor
    c. A shorted ignition switch
    d. High resistance in the motor switch

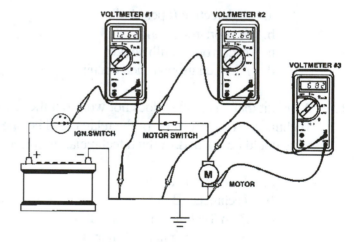

18. A convertible top will not operate either up or down. The relay(s) does not click when the switch is depressed. Technician A says that the switch could be defective. Technician B says that the electric pump motor for the power convertible top could be defective. Which technician is correct?

    a. Technician A only
    b. Technician B only
    c. Both Technicians A and B
    d. Neither Technician A nor B

19. The circuit shown is being tested at various points using a voltmeter. Technician A says that the battery voltage is 4.0 volts. Technician B says that there must be a poor ground connection or loose connection on the battery. Which technician is correct?

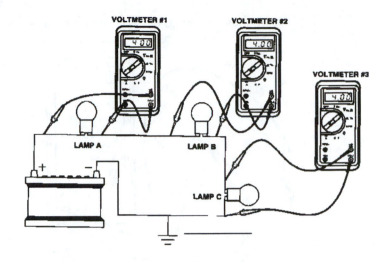

   a. Technician A only
   b. Technician B only
   c. Both Technicians A and B
   d. Neither Technician A nor B

20. The fuse to the cigarette lighter keeps blowing. What is the *most likely* cause?

   a. High resistance in the heater element of the lighter
   b. Corrosion on the electrical connector to the lights
   c. A short to ground
   d. Poor lighter socket ground

21. What is the meter measuring?

   a. Resistance of the ECT sensor
   b. Voltage signal of the ECT sensor
   c. Voltage output from the PCM
   d. Resistance of the electrical connector

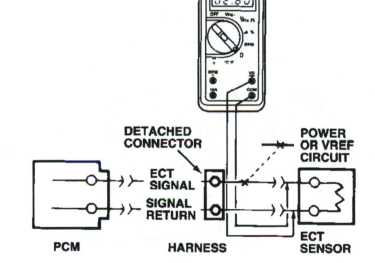

22. The windshield wiper operates too slowly at times even when set to the high-speed position. This fault can be caused by all of the following *except* _____.

   a. High resistance in the wiper circuit
   b. A blown fuse
   c. Excessive voltage drop in the power side of the circuit
   d. A poor electrical ground connector

18

23. The meter shown reads OL. Technician A says that this means that the meter leads are defective. Technician B says that this means that the resistance between the test leads is greater than the meter can measure. Which technician is correct?

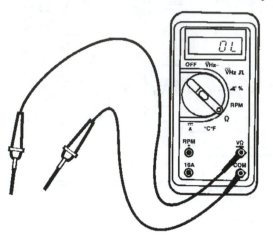

   a. Technician A only
   b. Technician B only
   c. Both Technicians A and B
   d. Neither Technician A nor B

24. An inoperative horn is being diagnosed. Technician A says that a fused jumper wire can be attached to the positive terminal of the battery at one end and the horn terminal at the other end to check if the horn works. Technician B says that checking for voltage at the horn terminal will verify that the horn itself is at fault if battery voltage is available when the horn button is pushed. Which technician is correct?

   a. Technician A only
   b. Technician B only
   c. Both Technicians A and B
   d. Neither Technician A nor B

25. The electrical connector is being tested in the circuit shown. The meter indicates 0.0 volts on the display. What is the *most likely* cause?

   a. Normal for a good connector
   b. Corroded terminals inside the connector
   c. Open circuit
   d. Battery is completely discharged

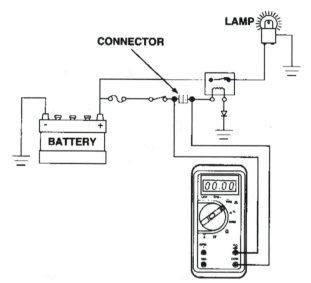

26. A relay is being checked out of the vehicle using a DMM. Technician A says that the coil winding can be checked by selecting the DC volt setting. Technician B says that the coil should measure OL on the meter if the relay is OK. Which technician is correct?

   a. Technician A only
   b. Technician B only
   c. Both Technicians A and B
   d. Neither Technician A nor B

27. A light circuit containing a relay as shown is being tested using two voltmeters. Technician A says the relay diode must be blown open. Technician B says the relay contacts must be electrically open. Which technician is correct?

    a. Technician A only
    b. Technician B only
    c. Both Technicians A and B
    d. Neither Technician A nor B

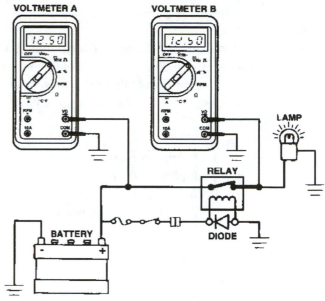

28. One rear taillight does not work and a test light is being used to check for voltage at a taillight socket. Technician A says that the alligator clip on the test light should be attached to a good ground before testing. Technician B says that the lights should be turned on before testing the socket terminal. Which technician is correct?

    a. Technician A only
    b. Technician B only
    c. Both Technicians A and B
    d. Neither Technician A nor B

29. A circuit containing a relay, switch, and lamp is being tested. The meter reading indicates 0.0 volts. What is the *most likely* cause?

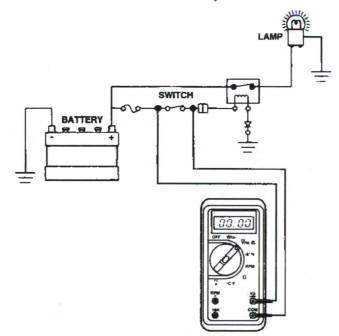

    a. Normal (good switch)
    b. A shorted diode in the relay circuit
    c. The relay contacts are electrically open
    d. A blown fuse

30. Two technicians are discussing performing a wire repair to a broken wire under the hood. Technician A says that the wire should be soldered and the splice covered with electrical tape. Technician B says that the wire should be soldered and covered with a heat-shrink tubing that contains an adhesive inside to seal against the weather. Which technician is correct?

    a. Technician A only
    b. Technician B only
    c. Both Technicians A and B
    d. Neither Technician A nor B

Electrical/Electronic Systems (A6)

B. Battery Diagnosis and Service Questions

31. Technician A says that a shorted diode in a generator (alternator) can discharge a battery. Technician B says that dirt on the battery can cause it to discharge. Which technician is correct?

    a. Technician A only
    b. Technician B only
    c. Both Technicians A and B
    d. Neither Technician A nor B

32. Whenever jump starting a disabled vehicle with another vehicle, what procedure should be followed?

    a. The last connection should be the positive (+) post of the dead battery
    b. The last connection should be the engine block of the disabled vehicle
    c. The generator (alternator) must be disconnected on both vehicles
    d. The ignition on both vehicles should be in the on (run) position

33. A fully charged 12-volt battery should indicate _____.

    a. 12.6 volts or higher
    b. A specific gravity of 1.265 or higher
    c. 12 volts
    d. Both a and b

34. A battery high-rate discharge (load capacity) test is being performed on a 12-volt battery. Technician A says that a good battery should have a voltage reading of higher than 9.6 volts while under load at the end of the 15-second test. Technician B says that the battery should be discharged (loaded to two times its CCA rating). Which technician is correct?

    a. Technician A only
    b. Technician B only
    c. Both Technicians A and B
    d. Neither Technician A nor B

35. When charging a maintenance-free battery _____.

    a. The initial charging rate should be about 35 amperes for 30 minutes
    b. The battery may not accept a charge for several hours, yet may still be a good (serviceable) battery
    c. The battery temperature should not exceed 125° F (hot to the touch)
    d. All of the above

36. Normal key-off battery drain (parasitic draw) on a vehicle with many computer and electronic circuits is _____.

    a. 20 - 30 milliamperes
    b. 2 - 3 amperes
    c. 0.20 to 0.40 A
    d. 150 to 300 milliamperes

37. A vehicle being tested has a key-off battery drain that exceeds specifications. Technician A says that the fuses should be removed one at a time until the excessive drain is eliminated thereby pinpointing the circuit. Technician B says a short finder should be used to locate the source of the draw. Which technician is correct?

    a. Technician A only
    b. Technician B only
    c. Both Technicians A and B
    d. Neither Technician A nor B

38. Technician A says that disconnecting a battery can cause driveability problems on some vehicles after the battery has been reconnected. Technician B says that disconnecting a battery can cause radio station presets to be lost. Which technician is correct?

    a. Technician A only
    b. Technician B only
    c. Both Technicians A and B
    d. Neither Technician A nor B

39. A customer arrives at a shop and his battery voltage is measured to be 13.6 volts with the engine off. What is the *most likely* result?

    a. The generator is overcharging the battery
    b. The generator is undercharging the battery
    c. Normal surface charge
    d. The battery is sulfated

40. A battery is being tested using a hydrometer. The readings are 1.265, 1.255, 1.260, 1.250, 1.260, and 1.265. Technician A says the battery is OK. Technician B says the battery is defective because the hydrometer readings are more than 0.005 between the highest and the lowest reading. Which technician is correct?

    a. Technician A only
    b. Technician B only
    c. Both Technicians A and B
    d. Neither Technician A nor B

41. The owner of a vehicle has a habit of leaving the lights on when parked at work requiring that the battery be jump-started every evening. Technician A says that this deep cycling of the battery could reduce the life of a battery. Technician B says that this practice can cause harm to the generator (alternator). Which technician is correct?

    a. Technician A only
    b. Technician B only
    c. Both Technicians A and B
    d. Neither Technician A nor B

42. Technician A says that a battery should not be stored on a concrete floor. Technician B says that a battery will not be able to be fully charged if placed on a concrete floor when being charged. Which technician is correct?

    a. Technician A only
    b. Technician B only
    c. Both Technicians A and B
    d. Neither Technician A nor B

43. A customer states that the starter will not crank the engine on Monday after the vehicle has remained parked since Friday evening. Technician A says that key-off battery drain (parasitic draw) test should be performed. Technician B says the battery should be charged and load tested. Which technician is correct?

    a. Technician A only
    b. Technician B only
    c. Both Technicians A and B
    d. Neither Technician A nor B

44. A new battery is being installed in a vehicle. The technician noticed that a large spark occurred between the battery post and the cable end as the last connection was being completed. Technician A says that this is normal. Technician B says that there could be an electrical drain on the battery such as a trunk light or interior light on as the last connection was being completed. Which technician is correct?

    a. Technician A only
    b. Technician B only
    c. Both Technicians A and B
    d. Neither Technician A nor B

Electrical/Electronic Systems (A6)

C. Starting System Diagnosis and Repair Questions

45. A starter motor is drawing too many amperes (current). Technician A says that this could be due to low battery voltage. Technician B says that it could be due to a defective starter motor. Which technician is correct?

    a. Technician A only
    b. Technician B only
    c. Both Technicians A and B
    d. Neither Technician A nor B

46. The starter solenoid makes a clicking noise when the ignition key is turned to the start position. A probable cause is _____.

    a. Low battery voltage
    b. A defective hold-in coil in the solenoid
    c. Poor connections at the battery
    d. All of the above

47. A starter cranks for a while, then whines. Technician A says that the starter solenoid may be bad. Technician B says that the starter drive may be bad. Which technician is correct?

    a. Technician A only
    b. Technician B only
    c. Both Technicians A and B
    d. Neither Technician A nor B

48. A driver turns the ignition switch to "start" and nothing happens (the dome light remains bright). Technician A says a discharged battery could be the cause. Technician B says that an *open* control circuit such as a defective neutral safety switch could be the cause. Which technician is correct?

    a. Technician A only
    b. Technician B only
    c. Both Technicians A and B
    d. Neither Technician A nor B

49. Slow cranking by the starter can be caused by all *except* _____.

    a. A low or discharged battery
    b. Corroded or dirty battery cable connections
    c. Engine mechanical problems
    d. An open solenoid pull-in winding

50. A starter motor turns slowly when the engine is being cranked. Technician A says that a positive battery cable with greater than 0.5 volt voltage drop could be the cause. Technician B says that a defective (high resistance) negative battery cable could be the cause. Which technician is correct?

    a. Technician A only
    b. Technician B only
    c. Both Technicians A and B
    d. Neither Technician A nor B

51. All of the following could be a cause of excessive starter ampere draw *except* _____.

    a. A misadjusted starter pinion gear
    b. A loose starter housing
    c. Armature wires separated from the commutator
    d. A bent armature

52. The starter motor armature has been rubbing on the pole shoes. The probable cause is _____.

    a. A bent starter shaft
    b. A worn commutator on the armature
    c. Worn starter bushing(s)
    d. Both a and c

53. Technician A says that high resistance in the cables or connections can cause rapid clicking of the solenoid. Technician B says that a battery must be 75% charged for accurate testing of the starting and charging systems. Which technician is correct?

    a. Technician A only
    b. Technician B only
    c. Both Technicians A and B
    d. Neither Technician A nor B

54. A rebuilt starter turns but will not disengage from the flywheel. The *most likely* cause is _____.

    a. A missing solenoid plunger return spring
    b. A defective starter drive
    c. The shift fork installed backward
    d. The solenoid contact installed backward

55. Technician A says a high-scale ammeter can be used to test the current draw of a starting circuit. Technician B says a high-scale voltmeter can be used to test the current draw of a starting circuit. Which technician is correct?

    a. Technician A only
    b. Technician B only
    c. Both Technicians A and B
    d. Neither Technician A nor B

56. A starter makes a grinding noise. Which is the *least likely* cause?

    a. A defective starter drive
    b. A defective flywheel
    c. Incorrect distance between the starter pinion and the flywheel
    d. Worn starter brushes

57. A technician connects one lead of a digital voltmeter to the positive (+) terminal of the battery and the other meter lead to the B terminal of the starter solenoid and then cranks the engine. During cranking, the voltmeter displays a reading of 878 mV. Technician A says that this reading indicates that the positive battery cable or cable end has too high resistance. Technician B says that this reading indicates that the starter is defective. Which technician is correct?

    a. Technician A only
    b. Technician B only
    c. Both Technician A and B
    d. Neither Technician A nor B

58. A vehicle equipped with a V-8 engine does not crank fast enough to start and sparks are observed at the negative terminal of the battery during cranking. Technician A says the battery could be discharged or defective. Technician B says that the negative cable is loose at the battery. Which technician is correct?

    a. Technician A only
    b. Technician B only
    c. Both Technician A and B
    d. Neither Technician A nor B

59. Battery voltage reads 10.32 volts on a DMM during engine cranking. Technician A says that the battery could be weak. Technician B says the starter may be defective. Which technician is correct?

    a. Technician A only
    b. Technician B only
    c. Both Technicians A and B
    d. Neither Technician A nor B

Electrical/Electronic Systems (A6)

D. Charging System Diagnosis and Repair Questions

60. A generator (alternator) is *not* charging. Technician A says that the voltage regulator could be defective. Technician B says the generator (alternator) brushes may be defective. Which technician is correct?

    a. Technician A only
    b. Technician B only
    c. Both Technicians A and B
    d. Neither Technician A nor B

61. The charging voltage of 12.4 volts is the same as the battery voltage. With the engine off, 0.0 volts is measured at the BAT terminal of the generator (alternator). Technician A says the generator (alternator) is defective. Technician B says the fusible link or generator output fuse is blown. Which technician is correct?

    a. Technician A only
    b. Technician B only
    c. Both Technicians A and B
    d. Neither Technician A nor B

62. An acceptable charging circuit voltage on a 12-volt system is _____.

    a. 13.5 to 15.0 volts
    b. 12.6 to 15.6 volts
    c. 12 to 14 volts
    d. 14.9 to 16.1 volts

63. A dead battery is being diagnosed and it was discovered that the charging voltage is 12.6 volts. Technician A says that the generator (alternator) is defective. Technician B says that the battery may be defective. Which technician is correct?

    a. Technician A only
    b. Technician B only
    c. Both Technicians A and B
    d. Neither Technician A nor B

64. Technician A says that a voltage-drop test of the charging circuit should be performed when current is flowing through the circuit. Technician B says to connect the leads of a voltmeter to the positive and negative terminals of the battery to measure the voltage drop of the charging system. Which technician is correct?

    a. Technician A only
    b. Technician B only
    c. Both Technicians A and B
    d. Neither Technician A nor B

65. Technician A says that a loose accessory drive belt or defective belt tensioner can cause the generator (alternator) to produce less than normal output. Technician B says that a poor ground connection on the generator case can cause lower generator output. Which technician is correct?

    a. Technician A only
    b. Technician B only
    c. Both Technicians A and B
    d. Neither Technician A nor B

66. A generator (alternator) is producing lower than the specified charging voltage. Which is the *least likely* cause?

    a. The battery is weak or defective
    b. The engine speed is not high enough during testing
    c. The drive belt is loose or slipping
    d. Cold outside temperature

67. A technician is checking the charging system for low output. A voltage drop of 1.67 volts is found between the generator (alternator) output terminal and the battery positive terminal. Technician A says that a corroded connector could be the cause. Technician B says that a defective rectifier diode could be the cause of the voltage drop. Which technician is correct?

    a. Technician A only
    b. Technician B only
    c. Both Technicians A and B
    d. Neither Technician A nor B

68. A charge light is on, but dim. What is the *most likely* cause?

    a. A defective rectifier bridge
    b. A defective diode trio
    c. A defective rotor
    d. Worn brushes

69. A fusible link between the battery and generator (alternator) is hot to the touch. The charging system voltage is 9.8 volts. What is the *most likely* cause?

    a. Overcharging
    b. Undercharging
    c. High resistance in the fusible link
    d. A poor battery ground

70. A generator is noisy. What is the *least likely* cause?

    a. A defective or loose drive belt
    b. A defective rectifier diode
    c. A defective bearing
    d. Worn brushes

71. A generator diode is being tested using a digital multimeter set to the diode check position. A good diode will read _____ if the leads are connected one way across the diode and _____ if the leads are reversed.

    a. 300; 300
    b. 0.575; 0.575
    c. OL; OL
    d. 0.651; OL

Electrical/Electronic Systems (A6)

E. Lighting Systems Diagnosis and Repair Questions

72. When the parking lamps are on and the turn signal is flashing, the side marker lamp alternates flashes with the turn signal. What is the *most likely* cause?

   a. An open bulb
   b. An open turn signal switch
   c. A blown parking light fuse
   d. Normal operation

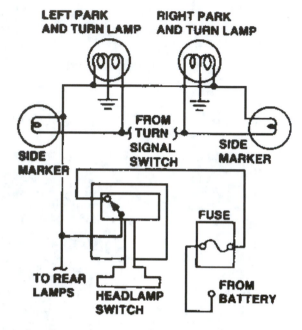

73. The headlamp on the left side of the vehicle is dim and yellow when turned on. The right side headlamp is bright and normal in color. Which is the *least likely* cause?

   a. Right side has more current
   b. Right side is normal
   c. Left side has more resistance
   d. Left side has a bad sealed beam

74. The high beam indicator on the dash does not come on but both headlight beams work. Technician A says that the indicator bulb could be defective. Technician B says the dimmer switch could be defective. Which technician is correct?

    a. Technician A only
    b. Technician B only
    c. Both Technicians A and B
    d. Neither Technician A nor B

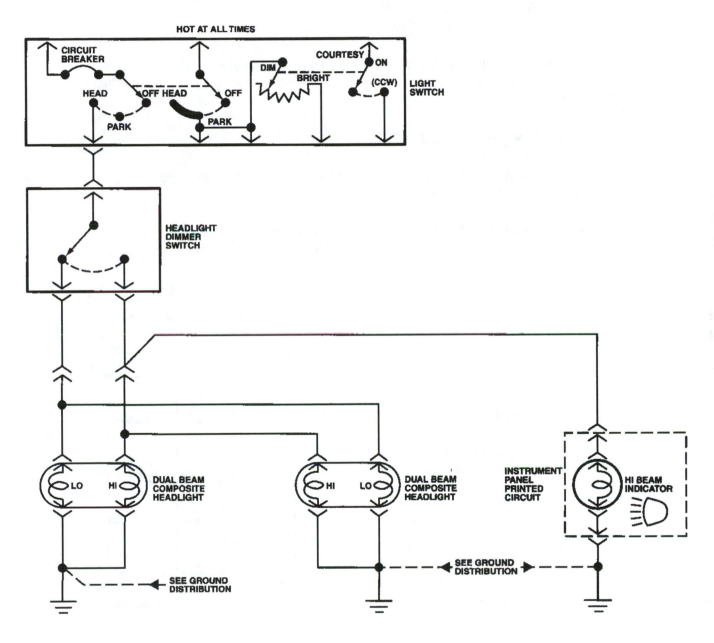

75. The left turn signal indicator light on the dash lights dimly whenever the parking or headlights are on, even though the turn signal is off. Technician A says that the most likely cause is a short circuit in the steering column. Technician B says that a common cause is a poor ground at the left front parking light. Which technician is correct?

    a. Technician A only
    b. Technician B only
    c. Both Technicians A and B
    d. Neither Technician A nor B

76. A customer complains that the life of the halogen headlight bulbs is only two weeks. Several different brands have been tried with the same results. What is the *most likely* cause?

    a. Poor ground at the headlights
    b. Shorted headlight switch
    c. The new bulbs were touched with bare hands during installation
    d. The bulbs were installed backwards

77. The fuse #7 shown is blown. Technician A says that the headlights will not work. Technician B says the taillights and parking lights will not work. Which technician is correct?

    a. Technician A only
    b. Technician B only
    c. Both Technicians A and B
    d. Neither Technician A nor B

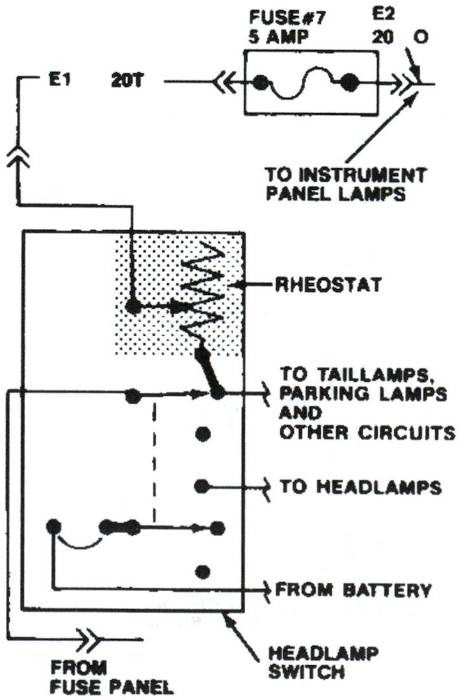

78. Two technicians are discussing a turn signal switch. Technician A says that a faulty turn signal switch could prevent the brake lights from working. Technician B says that a faulty brake switch will prevent the proper operation of the turn signals. Which technician is correct?

    a. Technician A only
    b. Technician B only
    c. Both Technicians A and B
    d. Neither Technician A nor B

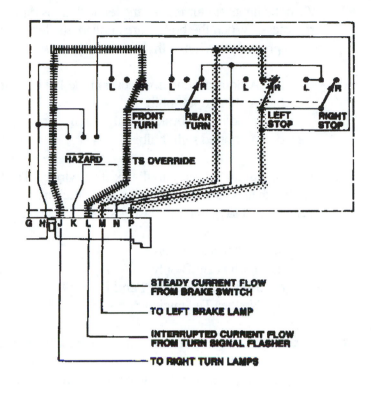

79. A corroded light socket could *most likely* cause _____.

    a. A fuse to blow in the circuit
    b. The light to be dim as a result of reduced current flow
    c. A feedback to occur to another circuit
    d. Damage to occur to the bulb as a result of decreased voltage

80. The right-side high beam does not work. The other lights on the vehicle function normally. What is the *most likely* cause?

    a. A defective dimmer switch
    b. A defective headlight
    c. A defective headlight ground
    d. A discharged battery

81. A vehicle's reverse lights are always on, even in "drive." What is the *most likely* cause?

    a. A misadjusted neutral safety switch
    b. An open neutral safety switch
    c. One of the reverse light bulbs has been installed backward
    d. The wrong bulb was installed for the reverse lights

82. When the lights are turned on, the left taillight is dim while the right taillight is a normal brightness. When the brakes are applied, the left light totally goes out, while the right side works properly. What is the *most likely* cause?

    a. A poor ground connector at the left bulb socket
    b. A shorted left bulb
    c. A defective brake pedal switch
    d. A shorted right bulb

83. Trailer lights are spliced into the existing wiring. The turn indicator lights on the dash flash rapidly when a turn signal is activated. Technician A says that the wiring must be reversed. Technician B says that the flasher should be changed. Which technician is correct?

    a. Technician A only
    b. Technician B only
    c. Both Technicians A and B
    d. Neither Technician A nor B

84. A defective taillight or front turn signal/park light bulb could cause _____.

    a. The turn signal indicator on the dash to light when the lights are turned on
    b. The dash lights to come on when the brake lights are on
    c. The lights-on warning chime sounds if the brake pedal is depressed
    d. All of the above

85. A defective brake switch could prevent proper operation of the _____.

    a. Cruise control
    b. ABS brakes
    c. Shift interlock
    d. All of the above

86. The headlights failed on a vehicle. A melted dimmer switch was found during a visual inspection. Technician A says that high output headlight bulbs might have been installed causing the switch to fail. Technician B says that adding auxiliary lights in parallel with the headlights could be the cause. Which technician is correct?

    a. Technician A only
    b. Technician B only
    c. Both Technicians A and B
    d. Neither Technician A nor B

Electrical/Electronic Systems (A6)

F. Gauges, Warning Devices, and Driver Information Systems Diagnosis and Repair Questions

87. Two technicians are discussing a fuel gauge. Technician A says that a corroded connection at the fuel tank sending unit will cause the fuel gauge to read lower or higher than normal. Technician B says that if the connector to the fuel tank sending unit is disconnected from the tank unit (ignition on), the fuel gauge should go to full or empty depending on the vehicle. Which technician is correct?

   a. Technician A only
   b. Technician B only
   c. Both Technicians A and B
   d. Neither Technician A nor B

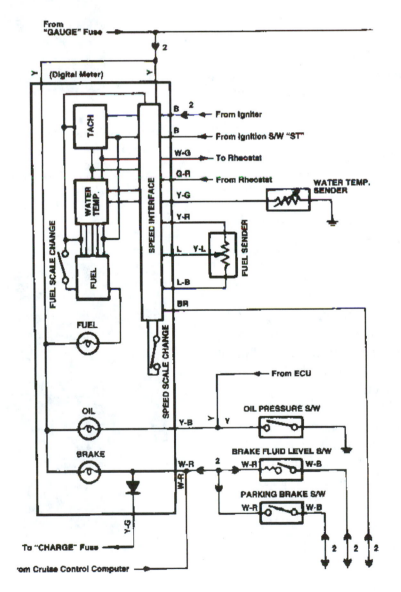

88. A brake warning lamp on the dash remains on whenever the ignition is on. If the wire to the pressure differential switch (usually a part of a combination valve or built into the master cylinder) is unplugged, the dash lamp goes out. Technician A says that this is an indication of a hydraulic brake problem. Technician B says that the problem is probably due to a stuck parking brake cable switch. Which technician is correct?

   a. Technician A only
   b. Technician B only
   c. Both Technicians A and B
   d. Neither Technician A nor B

89. The charge light does not come on when the key is turned to the "run" position. What is the *most likely* cause?

   a. A blown (melted) generator output fusible link
   b. A burned-out bulb
   c. A defective diode in the generator (alternator)
   d. A short inside the generator (alternator)

90. The left turn signal indicator on the instrument panel stays on and does not flash. The right side signal functions properly. What is the *most likely* cause?

   a. A defective flasher
   b. A bad bulb
   c. A defective turn signal switch
   d. Low battery voltage

91. A vehicle comes in with a nonfunctioning gas gauge. When the sending unit wire is disconnected and grounded, the gauge reading goes to "full." Technician A says this proves that the gauge is okay. Technician B says this proves that the sending unit is bad. Which technician is correct?

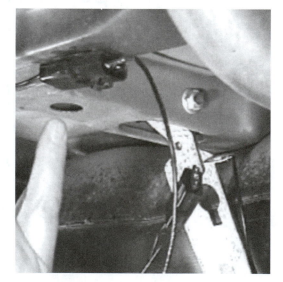

   a. Technician A only
   b. Technician B only
   c. Both Technicians A and B
   d. Neither Technician A nor B

92. If an oil pressure warning lamp on a vehicle is on all the time, yet the engine oil pressure is normal, what is the *most likely* cause?

   a. A defective (shorted) oil pressure sending unit (sensor)
   b. A shorted dash warning light
   c. An open wire between the sending unit (sensor) and the dash warning lamp
   d. Clogged oil pump passage(s)

93. A customer wanted to increase the size of tires on a pickup truck. Technician A says that a larger diameter tire will decrease the calculated fuel economy. Technician B says the larger tires will cause the speedometer to read faster than the actual speed. Which technician is correct?

   a. Technician A only
   b. Technician B only
   c. Both Technicians A and B
   d. Neither Technician A nor B

94. The coolant temperature gauge reads low (cold) all of the time. Which is the *least likely* cause?

   a. A defective coolant temperature sensor or circuit
   b. A defective dash gauge
   c. An engine thermostat stuck open
   d. Too much antifreeze in the coolant

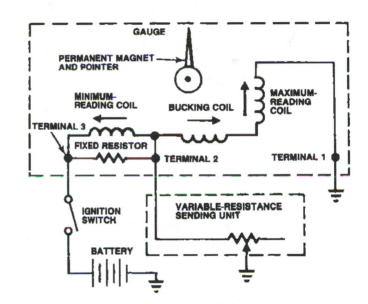

95. The left side turn signal indicator light on the dash blinks rapidly when the left side turn signals are turned on, but the right side flashes normally when the right side turn signals are turned on. What is the *most likely* cause?

   a. A defective flasher unit
   b. Burned out right front parking lamp bulb
   c. Burned out taillight bulb on the left side
   d. A shorted brake switch

Electrical/Electronic Systems (A6)

G. Horn and Wiper/Washer Diagnosis and Repair Questions

96. What does the adjustment screw do on the horn as shown?

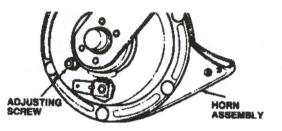

   a. Adjusts the volume
   b. Adjusts the frequency
   c. Adjusts to clear up the quality (tone) of the horn
   d. Adjusts the voltage of the horn

97. One horn out of the two on the vehicle does not work. Technician A says that a poor ground connection on the horn that does not work could be the cause. Technician B says that an open in the horn contact ring in the steering column could be the cause. Which technician is correct?

   a. Technician A only
   b. Technician B only
   c. Both Technicians A and B
   d. Neither Technician A nor B

98. A horn relay is being checked using a DMM set to read ohms. Technician A says the relay being tested is OK. Technician B says the relay being tested is defective (open). Which technician is correct?

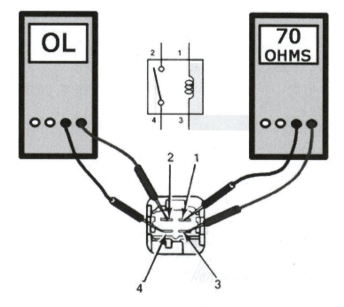

   a. Technician A only
   b. Technician B only
   c. Both Technicians A and B
   d. Neither Technician A nor B

99. A vehicle is equipped with one horn and it sounds garbled and very weak. Technician A says that the horn could be defective. Technician B says that the horn retaining bolt may be loose. Which technician is correct?

   a. Technician A only
   b. Technician B only
   c. Both Technicians A and B
   d. Neither Technician A nor B

100. A horn blows all the time and cannot be shut off unless the wire(s) to the horn is removed. What is the *most likely* cause?

    a. An open horn relay
    b. The horn wire in the steering column is shorted to ground
    c. A poor ground on the horn
    d. A defective horn

101. The horn does not work but the horn relay can be heard to click whenever the horn is depressed on the steering wheel. Which is the *least likely* cause?

    a. The horn wire in the steering column is shorted to ground
    b. The relay contacts are corroded
    c. A defective horn
    d. An open horn ground connection

102. The windshield wipers work OK until the headlights or the blower motor are turned on and then the wipers slow down to about half normal speed. What is the *most likely* cause?

    a. Worn brushes in the wiper motor
    b. A weak battery
    c. A defective wiper switch
    d. A poor body-to-engine ground

103. A two-speed wiper system is being diagnosed. The wipers work on high only and do not operate at all on low or delay positions. Technician A says that a defective wiper motor could be the cause. Technician B says that a poor ground could be the cause. Which technician is correct?

    a. Technician A only
    b. Technician B only
    c. Both Technicians A and B
    d. Neither Technician A nor B

104. The wipers will not go to the park position but simply stop where they are when the switch or ignition is turned off. Technician A says a poor ground for the wipers could be the cause. Technician B says that the motor assembly may need to be replaced. Which technician is correct?

    a. Technician A only
    b. Technician B only
    c. Both Technicians A and B
    d. Neither Technician A nor B

105. The engine cooling fan does not operate. Technician A says a blown fusible link could be the cause. Technician B says that a defective engine fan relay could be the cause. Which technician is correct?

     a. Technician A only
     b. Technician B only
     c. Both Technicians A and B
     d. Neither Technician A nor B

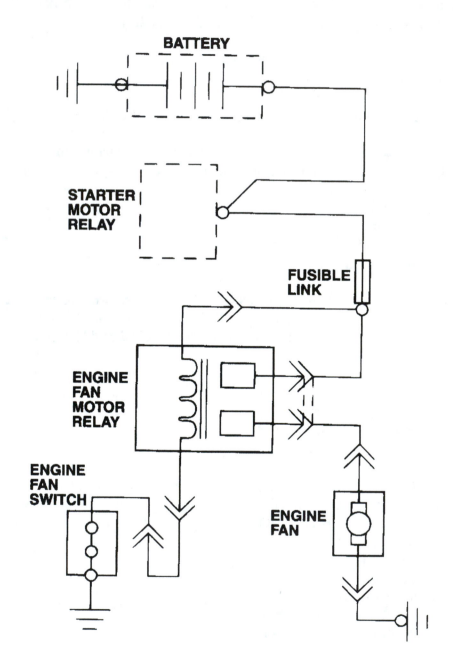

106. If an open occurred at terminal #28 of the high/low relay, what is the *most likely* result?

   a. High-speed operation only
   b. The wipers will not operate at any speed
   c. The 15 A fuse will blow when the wipers are tuned on
   d. Low-speed operation only

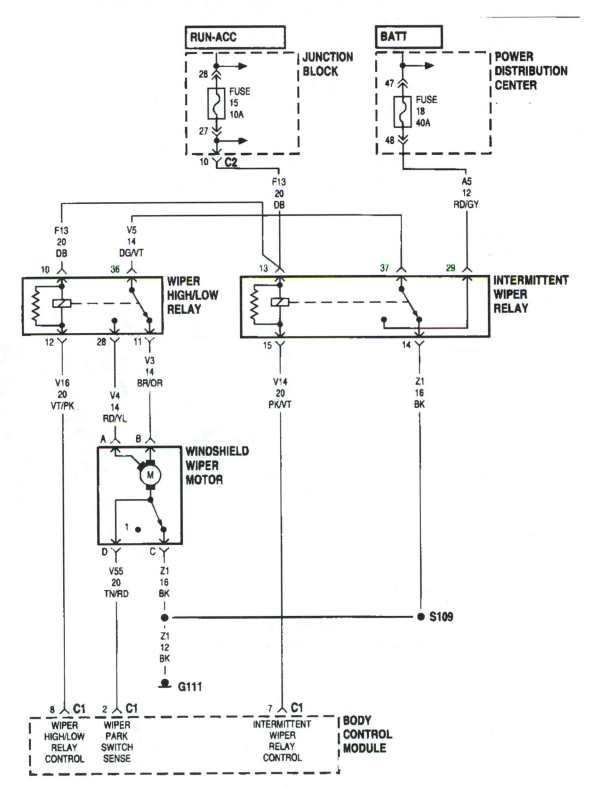

Electrical/Electronic Systems (A6)

H. Accessories Diagnosis and Repair Questions

107. A radio operates okay on FM but does not receive AM signals. Which is the *least likely* cause?

    a. A defective antenna
    b. A defective radio
    c. A high resistance in power lead wires
    d. A poor ground connection on the antenna

108. The driver and passenger side airbags are being disabled as protection against the possibility of accidental deployment. The technician should look for electrical connectors that are what color?

    a. Red
    b. Yellow
    c. Black
    d. Green

109. A blower motor stopped working on all speeds. A technician tested the motor touching a jumper wire from the battery positive (+) terminal to the motor power terminal and the motor did run. Technician A says that the motor should be checked using a fused jumper lead to test for excessive current draw. Technician B says that the resistor pack and/or relay are likely to be defective. Which technician is correct?

    a. Technician A only
    b. Technician B only
    c. Both Technicians A and B
    d. Neither Technician A nor B

110. A blower motor is drawing more than the specified current. Technician A says that the blower motor ground connection could be corroded. Technician B says that the blower relay is shorted. Which technician is correct?

    a. Technician A only
    b. Technician B only
    c. Both Technicians A and B
    d. Neither Technician A nor B

111. An independent power window switch has a break in the power lead going to the switch. Technician A says the window will go up and down from the master, but not from the independent switch. Technician B says that the window will work okay from the master and only go down from the independent switch. Which technician is correct?

    a. Technician A only
    b. Technician B only
    c. Both Technicians A and B
    d. Neither Technician A nor B

112. The A/C compressor clutch does not engage. Technician A says that an open high pressure cutout switch could be the problem. Technician B says a blown compressor clutch diode could be the cause. Which technician is correct?

    a. Technician A only
    b. Technician B only
    c. Both Technicians A and B
    d. Neither Technician A nor B

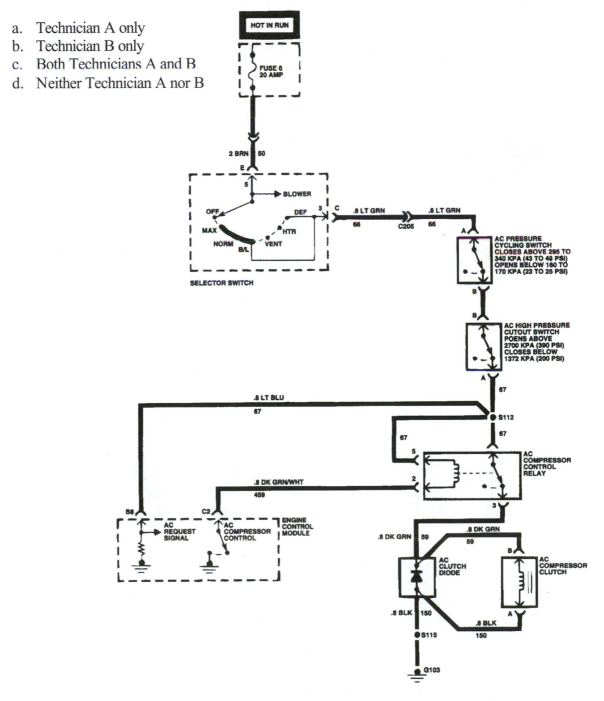

113. The cruise control stops working when the vehicle is being driven over bumpy roads but works OK on smooth roads. Technician A says that the brake switch could be misadjusted. Technician B says that this is a normal safety device to prevent the driver from speeding while traveling over bumpy roads. Which technician is correct?

    a. Technician A only
    b. Technician B only
    c. Both Technicians A and B
    d. Neither Technician A nor B

114. A technician is checking a headlight door motor with an ammeter. It shows excessive current draw. What is the *most likely* cause?

    a. A bad ground
    b. A binding headlight door
    c. A loose connection
    d. A blown fuse

115. A blower is running slow on all speeds. What is the *most likely* cause?

    a. A blown resistor
    b. Worn/dry bearings in the motor
    c. A bad fan switch
    d. Open ignition switch

116. A customer concern is that the radio has static on all radio stations. Technician A says the antenna should be checked for a proper ground connection. Technician B says to check the radio for a proper ground connection. Which technician is correct?

    a. Technician A only
    b. Technician B only
    c. Both Technicians A and B
    d. Neither Technician A nor B

117. If only one power door lock is inoperative, what is the *most likely* cause?

    a. A poor ground connection at the power door lock relay
    b. A defective motor (or solenoid)
    c. A defective (open) circuit breaker for the power circuit
    d. A defective (open) fuse for the control circuit

118. No sound is heard from the left rear speaker. What is the *most likely* cause?

    a. A defective audio unit
    b. Poor ground at G502
    c. An open antenna lead
    d. A defective speaker

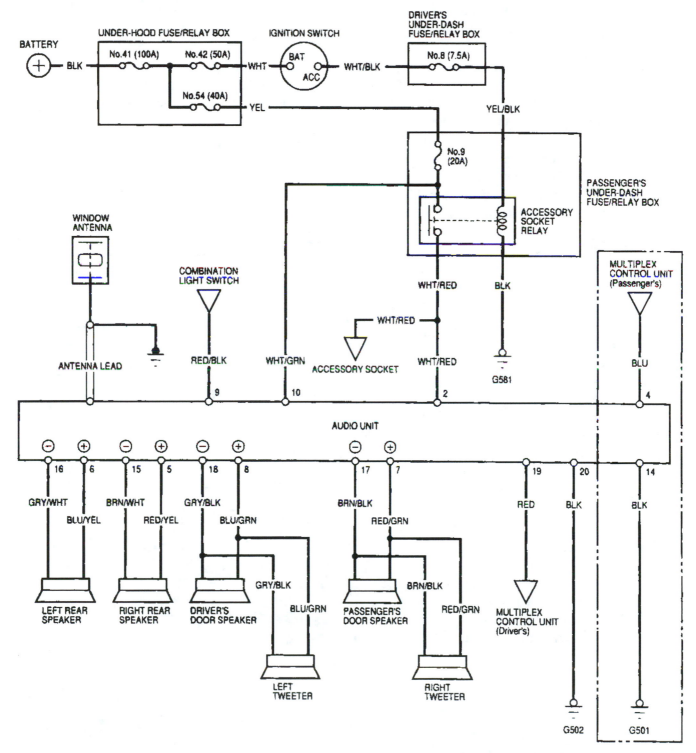

119. The trunk lid will not operate from the dash switch on the remote. Technician A says that a scan tool should be used to activate the trunk module to check whether the circuit can function. Technician B says to replace the dash switch. Which technician is correct?

    a. Technician A only
    b. Technician B only
    c. Both Technicians A and B
    d. Neither Technician A nor B

120. The blower motor operates at low speed regardless of the position selected on the blower motor switch. Technician A says an open thermal limiter could be the cause. Technician B says an open at the "LO" contact of the blower motor switch could be the cause. Which technician is correct?

    a. Technician A only
    b. Technician B only
    c. Both Technicians A and B
    d. Neither Technician A nor B

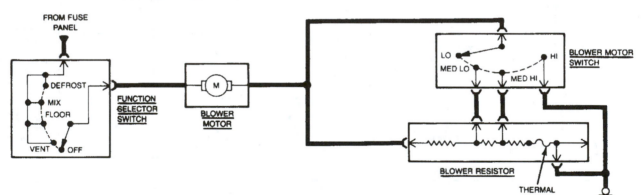

121. A rear window defogger is being tested using a DMM as shown. If the meter lead on the right is moved to the midpoint "c", what would a typical reading be for a properly operating defogger?

    a. About 12 volts
    b. About 6 volts
    c. Almost zero volts
    d. OL

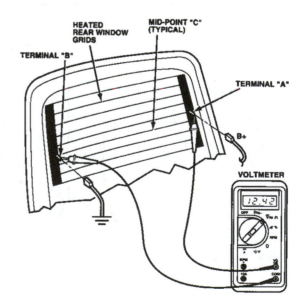

122. The indicating light bulb burned out in the circuit shown. Technician A says that the rear defogger will not work. Technician B says that the relay will not operate without the bulb in the circuit. Which technician is correct?

    a. Technician A only
    b. Technician B only
    c. Both Technicians A and B
    d. Neither Technician A nor B

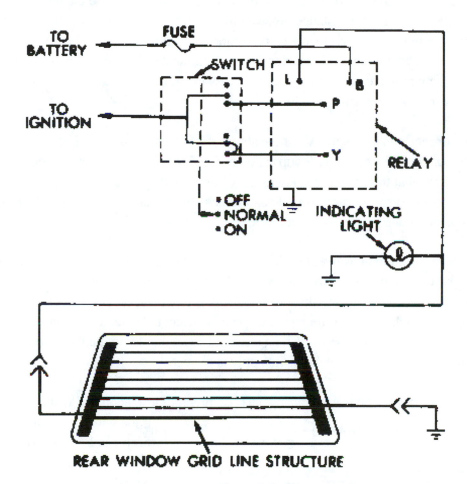

REAR WINDOW GRID LINE STRUCTURE

Electrical/Electronic Systems (A6)

A. General Electrical/Electronic System Diagnosis
Answers and Explanations

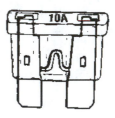

1. **The correct answer is c.** Both technicians are correct. Technician A is correct because a short to voltage will usually affect more than one circuit and depending on the resistance involved may or may not cause a fuse to blow. Technician B is correct because a short to ground involves a power side wire contacting ground, which reduces or eliminates the resistance in the circuit and will cause a fuse to blow. Answers **a, b, d** are not correct because both technicians are correct.

2. **The correct answer is d.** All of the above are correct. Answer **a** is correct because the customer concerns could be occurring on and off. Answer **b** is correct because there may be other faults that the customer is not aware of that could have an effect on the electrical fault. Answer **c** is correct because verbal communication and terminology could be misinterpreted by the customer and/or the service advisor.

3. **The correct answer is a.** Technician A is correct because using a fuse in the jumper wire will help protect against excessive current flow through the jumper lead if one end accidentally touches metal when the other end is attached to the circuit. Technician B is not correct because a switch, which should have little or no resistance, can be safely bypassed using a jumper wire without doing any harm to the circuit. However, an electrical *load* should not be bypassed. Answers **c** and **d** are not correct because Technician A only is correct.

4. **The correct answer is c.** A fusible link has fireproof insulation and will not burn or even discolor if the wire inside has melted. To check a

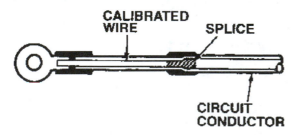

fusible link, simply pull on the ends to see if it stretches like a rubber band, which would indicate the wire inside has melted. Answer **a** is not correct because if the insulation has been cut, the fusible link must be replaced. Answer **b** is not correct because replacing a fusible link is not the proper method to use to check to see if it is blown. Answer **d** is not correct because a fusible link must be replaced if cut even if it was OK before the inspection.

5. **The correct answer is d.** The first step in any diagnostic procedure is to verify the customer concern because if the concern cannot be verified, the repair cannot be verified. Answer **a** is not correct because even though checking the hints and troubleshooting guidelines is an important step, it is not the first step. Answer **b** is not correct because even though the cause of the malfunction must be determined before it can be repaired, this is not the first step of the diagnostic procedure. Answer **c** is not correct even though a thorough visual inspection is an important part of the diagnostic procedure, it is not the first step.

6. **The correct answer is c.** Both technicians are correct. Technician A is correct because a test light will provide resistance and light as long as the circuit is shorted to ground. Technician B is correct because a circuit breaker will open if the current exceeds its rating to prevent any damage to the wiring from excessive current flow. When the fault has been disconnected, the circuit breaker will not trip indicating to the technician that the location of the fault has been found. Answer **d** is not correct because both technicians are correct.

7. **The correct answer is b.** The meter is connected in series in the circuit and the reduced amount of current through the circuit due to the corrosion on the lamp terminal would be indicated on the meter display. Answer **a** is not correct because the leads are attached to two parts of the circuit and there is power applied to the circuit. To measure resistance, the circuit must be open to prevent current from flowing, which could damage an ohmmeter. Answer **c** is not correct because the meter should be connected across a load or part of a circuit in parallel, not in series as shown. Answer **d** is not correct because to measure available voltage, the meter should be connected across the load in parallel and not in series as shown.

8. **The correct answer is c.** Both technicians are correct. Technician A is correct because if the ohmmeter display shows zero or low ohms, this means that there is little if any resistance between the meter leads. The component being tested has continuity and current will flow if connected to an electrical power source. Technician B is correct because an infinity reading, such as "OL" on the display, means that there is such a high resistance between the meter leads that the meter is unable to measure on the highest setting. In other words, the component being measured lacks continuity and no current will flow if connected to an electrical power source. Answer **d** is not correct because both technicians are correct.

9. **The correct answer is a.** A meter reading of OL means over limit or overload and indicates an open circuit. For all practical reasons, no electrical current will flow if connected to an electrical power source. Answer **b** is not correct because if the component is shorted, the meter will read low or zero ohms instead of OL. Answer **c** is not correct because a normal circuit should have some resistance instead of being open where no current will flow. Answer **d** is not correct because if the circuit or component has low resistance, the meter should display the value and not show that the component or circuit is electrically open.

10. **The correct answer is b.** With the meter set to read K ohms, the reading of 0.93 means that the resistance of the component being measured has 0.93 of a K ohm or 930 ohms. Answers **a, c,** and **d** are not correct because they are not slightly less than 1000 ohms.

11. **The correct answer is a.** A millivolt is one-thousandth of a volt or 1/1000 or 0.001. Therefore, 432 thousandths of a volt would be 0.432. Answers **b, c,** and **d** are not correct because they do not represent 432 millivolts.

12. **The correct answer is d.** A voltage drop should occur when current flows through an electrical load. If the voltage is the same on both sides of the load, such as a light bulb, this means that no current is flowing and an open circuit ground is the cause. Answer **a** (open bulb) is not correct because if the bulb were electrically open, voltage would not be available on both sides. Answer **b** is not correct because a short to ground would cause current to flow and the voltage would drop to zero or close to zero instead of remaining the same on both sides of the bulb. Answer **c** is not correct because if current were flowing through the bulb, there should be a difference in voltage across the bulb and a corroded socket. This could affect the brightness of the bulb but this is not important because there is no current flow.

13. **The correct answer is d.** Neither technician is correct. Technician A is not correct because the relay could not click if the coil winding, which creates the magnetic field needed to move the armature (movable contact) of the relay, were open. Technician B is not correct because a shorted relay coil could not create a magnetic field strong enough to cause the relay to click. Answers **a, b,** and **c** are not correct because neither technician is correct.

14. **The correct answer is a.** Technician A is correct because as current flows through an electrical load, the voltage drops. In this case, all three lamps must have the same resistance because each lamp dropped the voltage by 4 volts in this series circuit. Technician B is not correct because a drop in voltage when current flows through an electrical load is normal. Answers **c** and **d** are not correct because Technician A only is correct.

15. **The correct answer is d.** The valet switch in the glove compartment is used to disable the dash switch so that no unauthorized person can access the trunk. Only the valet key should be left to insure that this feature is effective to prevent the trunk from being unlocked. Answer **a** is not correct because the trunk operates from the remote indicating that the trunk release solenoid is functioning correctly. Answer **b** is not correct because the trunk release operates from the remote indicating that the release circuit is functioning OK. Answer **c** is not correct because a shorted switch would cause the trunk to release without being pressed rather than not functioning at all.

16. **The correct answer is a.** The technician should select DC (direct current) volts because most circuits in a vehicle use 12 volts and can be checked using the DC V position on the DMM. Answer **b** is not correct because even though DC A (amperes) can be used to check for current flow in a circuit, it is not used to check for the presence of electricity. Answer **c** (Ω) is not correct because even though the bulb can be tested using this position to see if the filament is OK, it cannot be used to check for the presence of electricity at the socket. Answer **d** is not correct because lights use DC and not AC.

17. **The correct answer is d.** The voltmeter readings indicate that less than 7 volts is available to operate the motor, yet the voltage is OK up to the motor switch. This indicates that there is high resistance (high voltage drop) either in the switch or the wiring from the switch to the motor. Answer **a** is not correct because only 6.82 volts is available to operate the motor and this indicates a high resistance fault in the circuit. Answer **b** is not correct because the electrical load (motor) should create the highest voltage drop and this is the case even though the motor has less available voltage than it should for proper operation.

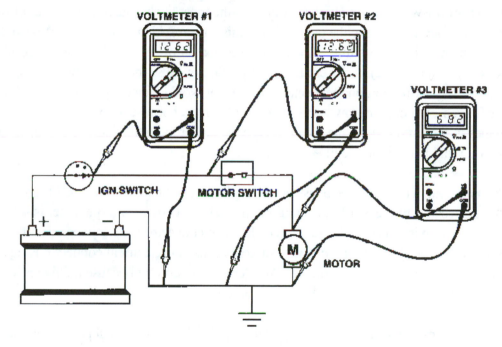

18. **The correct answer is a.** Technician A is correct because if the relay does not click, there is a fault in the control circuit that operates the coil of the relay and a defective switch could be the cause. Technician B is not correct because the relays do not operate to send electrical power to the motor. While the motor(s) could be defective, the fault is in the control circuit. Answers **c** and **d** are not correct because Technician A only is correct.

19. **The correct answer is d.**
Neither technician is correct.
Technician A is not correct
because the voltmeters are
measuring the difference in
voltage between the meter leads,
which indicates that the voltage
drop across each of the lamps is
4.0 volts. Technician B is not
correct because the sum (total)
of the voltage drop equals 12
volts indicating that there is little
if any resistance in the wiring or
the connection. Answer **c** is not correct because neither technician is correct.

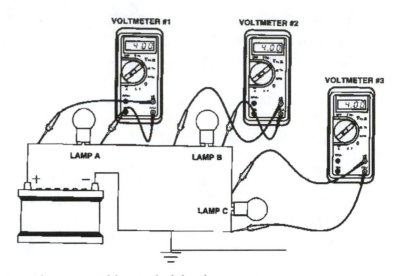

20. **The correct answer is c.** A short-to-ground is the most likely cause for a fuse to blow because
the electrical power will take the path of least resistance resulting in a rapid increase in the flow of
current, which will blow the fuse. Answer **a** is not correct because high resistance results in a
decrease (not an increase) in current flow and would not cause the fuse to blow. Answer **b** is not
correct because corrosion on the electrical connector would create high resistance and a decrease
(not an increase) in current flow. Answer **d** is not correct because a poor ground would cause
resistance in the circuit and while it could cause the lighter to not function correctly, the high
resistance would not cause the fuse to blow.

21. **The correct answer is a.** The resistance of engine coolant temperature (ECT) sensor is being
measured because the sensor has been disconnected from power and the meter is set to read
ohms. Answer **b** is not correct because the electrical connector is disconnected and the meter is
not set to read voltage. Answer **c** is not correct because the electrical connector is disconnected
and the meter is not set to read voltage. Answer **d** is not correct because the meter leads are
touching the sensor wires and not the connector terminals.

22. **The correct answer is b.** A blown fuse will stop the flow of electrical power and therefore the
wiper motor would not operate. Answers **a, c,** and **d** are not correct because each could be the
cause of a windshield wiper motor operating too slowly because each would reduce the current
flow through the motor.

23. **The correct answer is b.** Technician B is correct because OL (over limit) means that the
resistance between the leads exceeds the meter's capability. If the meter were auto ranging or set
to the highest resistance range, the OL indicates infinity resistance or an open circuit. Technician
A is not correct because even though the leads could be defective, the meter display still shows an
open circuit between the leads. Answers **c** and **d** are not correct because Technician B only is
correct.

24. **The correct answer is a.** Technician A is correct because a fused jumper wire attached to a horn should cause the horn to blow if the horn and the ground for the horn are OK. Technician B is not correct because even if 12 volts is available to the horn, the ground for the horn could be the fault and not the horn itself. Measuring 12 volts at the horn when the horn button is depressed would not indicate if there is excessive resistance in the horn circuit preventing enough current (amperes) to flow to the horn for proper operation. Answers **c** and **d** are not correct because Technician A only is correct.

25. **The correct answer is a.** The connector is being checked for a voltage drop with the circuit in operation. A zero reading indicates no resistance in the connector and indicates that it has no resistance. Answer **b** is not correct because corroded terminals would cause a voltage drop due to the resistance and the meter would read higher than zero voltage drop across the terminals of the connector. Answer **c** is not correct because the circuit is operating because the lamp is on. Answer **d** is not correct because the battery has enough voltage to light the lamp and the meter simply displays the voltage difference between the test leads and is not measuring the battery voltage.

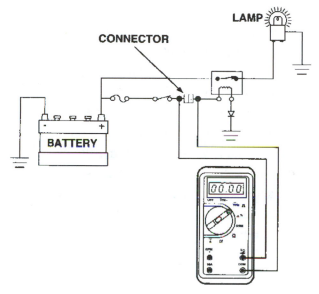

26. **The correct answer is d.** Neither technician is correct. Technician A is not correct because a coil of a relay should be checked on the ohms (resistance) setting on the DMM and not on the DC volt setting. Technician B is not correct because the relay coil should measure between 60 and 100 ohms for most relays and should not read OL (open circuit or over limit in the motor). Answers **a, b,** and **c** are not correct because neither technician is correct.

27. **The correct answer is d.** Neither technician is correct. Technician A is not correct because the meters are testing the voltage drop across the relay contacts and even though the diode may be blown, it cannot be determined by this test procedure. Technician B is not correct because there is voltage on both sides of the movable arm (contacts) of the relay, which indicates that the connector is closed without resistance and not open (infinity resistance). Answers **a, b,** and **c** are not correct because neither technician is correct.

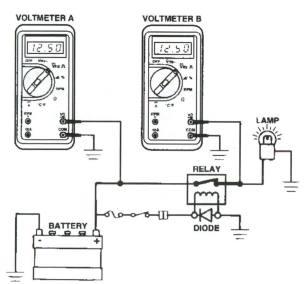

28. **The correct answer is c.** Both technicians are correct. Technician A is correct because a test light needs to be properly grounded to allow current to flow from the test point through the test light bulb and to ground. Technician B is correct because the taillights must be activated so that voltage can be checked at the taillight socket. Answers **a, b,** and **d** are not correct because both technicians are correct.

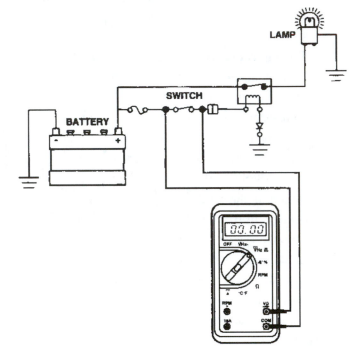

29. **The correct answer is a.** The meter is measuring the voltage drop across the switch and a zero reading indicates zero resistance and a good switch. Answer **b** is not correct because the meter cannot determine whether the diode is shorted with the leads attached to the switch. Answer **c** is not correct because the lamp is on, which indicates that the relay contacts must be electrically closed and not open. Answer **d** is not correct because if the fuse were blown (open circuit), the lamp would not be working.

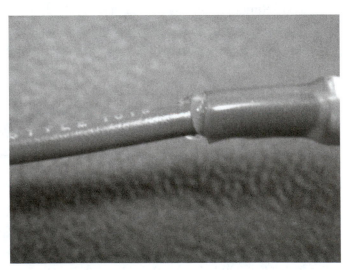

30. **The correct answer is b.** Technician B only is correct because all repaired wires under the hood (or under the vehicle) must be sealed to prevent moisture from getting into a splice where it could cause corrosion. A splice sleeve that contains adhesive inside can also be used to make a weather-proof wire repair. Technician A is not correct because electrical tape will not seal the splice from water, which could lead to corrosion and high resistance in the circuit. Answers **c** and **d** are not correct because Technician B only is correct.

Electrical/Electronic Systems (A6)

B. Battery Diagnosis and Service Answers and Explanations

31. **The correct answer is c.** Both technicians are correct. Technician A is correct because a diode should block the flow of electricity from the battery into the generator and if a diode were shorted, current would be drained from the battery. Technician B is correct because dirt combined with moisture in the air can cause some electric current to flow between the terminal posts of the battery. Answers **a, b,** and **d** are not correct because both technicians are correct.

32. **The correct answer is b.** The last connection should be to the engine block or jump start terminal of the disabled vehicle because a spark will occur and this spark should be as far away as possible from the battery so as to not ignite the escaping gases. Answer **a** is not correct because if the last connection were made at or near the battery, there is a chance that the spark created could ignite the escaping gases. Answer **c** is not  correct because no harm will be done to the generator if the proper polarity is observed and therefore, the generators do not need to be disconnected. Answer **d** is not correct because the ignition on both vehicles should be off (not on) to prevent the possible damage that could occur to electronic devices from the spark that occurs when the last connection is completed.

33. **The correct answer is d.** A fully-charged 12-volt battery should read 12.6 or higher (answer **a**) and have a specific gravity of 1.260 to 1.280 (answer **b**). Answers **a** and **b** are not correct alone because both **a** and **b** are correct. Answer **c** is not correct because a fully-charged 12-volt battery will have 12.6 volts or higher.

34. **The correct answer is a.** Technician A only is correct because at the end of a battery load test, the battery voltage should be higher than 9.6 volts at room temperature. Technician B is not correct because the battery should be loaded to one-half (rather than 2 times) the CCA rating. Answers **c** and **d** are not correct because Technician A only is correct.

35. **The correct answer is d.** All of the above are correct. Answer **a** is correct because a high initial charge is usually necessary to start the chemical reaction inside the cells to make the electrolyte conductive so the battery can accept a charge. Answer **b** is correct because a battery may not accept a charge, if totally discharged, until the electrolyte becomes conductive. Answer **c** is correct because temperature above 125°F (hot to the touch) can warp plates inside the battery. Answers **a, b,** and **c** are not correct because all are correct.

36. **The correct answer is a.** It is normal for a vehicle to have a normal key-off battery drain of 20 to 30 mA (0.02 to 0.03 A). Answer **b** (2 to 3 amperes), answer **c** (0.2 to 0.4 A), and answer **d** (150 to 300 mA) are not correct because they are all much higher than the maximum allowable specification of 50 mA (0.05 A) as stated by most vehicle manufacturers.

37. **The correct answer is a.** Technician A only is correct because a key-off battery drain could be caused by many different components and circuits and removing fuses one at a time until the draw decreases to normal is the recommended method to use to locate the circuit causing the draw. Technician B is not correct because a short finder is used to locate a short-to-ground that causes enough current to flow to blow a fuse and not just enough to drain a battery. Answers **c** and **d** are not correct because Technician A only is correct.

38. **The correct answer is c.** Both technicians are correct. Technician A is correct because the computer stores learned idle speed and other engine operating parameters that will be lost when the battery is disconnected. Technician B is correct because the stored radio station presets will usually be lost if the battery is disconnected. Some anti-theft radios require that a code be entered after the battery has been reconnected to restore proper operation. Answers **a, b,** and **d** are not correct because both technicians are correct.

39. **The correct answer is c.** It is normal for the battery voltage to read over 13 volts after the engine is turned off due to the charging system voltage (13.5 to 15.0 V) causing a surface charge, which is quickly removed as soon as an electrical load is applied. Answer **a** is not correct because this test alone cannot determine whether the generator is overcharging the battery. Answer **b** is not correct because it is unlikely that the generator is undercharging the battery due to the surface charge on the battery when the engine stopped. Answer **d** is not correct because this test cannot determine whether the battery is sulfated.

40. **The correct answer is a.** Technician A only is correct because a good battery will display a hydrometer reading within 0.050 between the highest and lowest tested cell. A variation greater than 0.050 indicates a possible faulty battery. Technician B is not correct because the maximum allowable difference between cells of a battery during a hydrometer test is 0.05, not 0.005. Answers **c** and **d** are not correct because Technician A only is correct.

°C	°F	Correction
71C	160F	+32
65.5C	150F	+28
60C	140F	+24
54.5C	130F	+20
49C	120F	+16
43C	110F	+12
37.5C	100F	+ 8
32.5C	90F	+ 4
27C	80F	0
21C	70F	− 4
15.5C	60F	− 8
10C	50F	−12
4.5C	40F	−16
-1C	30F	−20
-6.5C	20F	−24
-12C	10F	−28

SUBTRACT | ADD

EXAMPLE:
HYDROMETER READING.............. 1.250
ELECTROLYTE TEMPERATURE......... 40F
SUBTRACT SPECIFIC GRAVITY....... −.016
CORRECTED SPECIFIC GRAVITY IS.... 1.234

EXAMPLE:
HYDROMETER READING.............. 1.240
ELECTROLYTE TEMPERATURE......... 100F
ADD SPECIFIC GRAVITY .... +.008
CORRECTED SPECIFIC GRAVITY IS.... 1.248

A FULLY CHARGED BATTERY HAS A SPECIFIC GRAVITY OF ABOUT 1.265.

41. **The correct answer is c.** Both technicians are correct. Technician A is correct because even though batteries are designed to withstand being deep cycled a few times, the constant discharge and recharge will drastically shorten the life of the battery. Technician B is correct because if the generator is always attempting to charge a battery that is fully discharged, harm can be done to the generator due to the constant charging without ever reaching the voltage regulator limit. Answers **a, b,** and **d** are not correct because both technicians are correct.

42. **The correct answer is a.** Technician A only is correct because while the battery cannot discharge through the plastic case, the concrete is cold and damp. If a battery is stored on concrete, the difference in temperature between the top and bottom of the cells causes the battery to self-discharge. All batteries should be stored in cool dry locations. Technician B is not correct because even though a battery may self-discharge if stored on concrete, it can be charged on concrete as long as it does not remain on the concrete floor in storage after it has been fully charged. Answers **c** and **d** are not correct because Technician A only is correct.

43. **The correct answer is c.** Both technicians are correct. Technician A is correct because an excessive key-off battery drain (parasitic draw) could cause the battery to become discharged during the weekend and be unable to crank the engine on Monday. Technician B is correct because the battery itself could have lost its ability to hold a charge or to provide enough cranking amperes to start the engine. Answers **a, b,** and **d** are not correct because both technicians are correct.

44. **The correct answer is b.** Technician B is correct because a spark indicates that an electrical load is causing current to flow from the battery as the last cable is attached. It is normal to see a small spark due to the electrical load on many small keep-alive or memory circuits, but a large spark is abnormal and the cause should be located and corrected to avoid discharging the battery. Technician A is not correct because even though a small spark is normal, a large spark indicates that an electrical device is conducting current and could discharge the battery if not corrected. Answers **c** and **d** are not correct because Technician B only is correct.

Electrical/Electronic Systems (A6)

C. Starting System Diagnosis and Repair Answers and Explanations

45. **The correct answer is c.** Both technicians are correct. Technician A is correct because low battery voltage causes the starter motor to rotate slower than normal and not produce the normal counter EMF (CEMF) that a starter would normally produce. Due to the reduced CEMF, the starter draws more than the normal amount of current from the battery. Technician B is correct because a defective starter will cause an increase in current from the battery. Answers **a, b,** and **d** are not correct because both technicians are correct.

46. **The correct answer is d.** All of the above are probable causes of a clicking solenoid including low battery voltage (answer **a**), defective hold-in winding coil in the solenoid (answer **b**), and poor connections at the battery (answer **c**). Low voltage is the usual cause of a clicking solenoid and low battery voltage or loose/corroded battery terminals are the most common causes. Answers **a, b,** and **c** are not correct because all are correct.

47. **The correct answer is b.** Technician B is correct because a worn starter drive will cause the starter motor to spin and not rotate the engine flywheel. Technician A is not correct because if the starter is rotating, the solenoid has to be working because the drive pinion is forced to mesh with the flywheel before current flows through the solenoid to the starter motor. Answers **c** and **d** are not correct because Technician B only is correct.

48. **The correct answer is b.** Technician B only is correct because an open in the control circuit, such as a neutral safety or clutch switch, will prevent the flow of electrical current to the starter solenoid and therefore, no current to the starter. If no current flows to the starter, the dome light will remain bright and no sound will be heard from the starter. Technician A is not correct because even though the battery is discharged, the solenoid should at least click and the voltage (as observed by looking at the dome light) should drop. Answers **c** and **d** are not correct because Technician B only is correct.

49. **The correct answer is d.** If the solenoid hold-in winding were open, the solenoid and the starter would not crank the engine at all and therefore, could not be the cause of slow cranking. Answers **a** (discharged battery), **b** (corroded battery cable connections), and **c** (engine mechanical problem) can all cause slow cranking.

50. **The correct answer is c.** Both technicians are correct. Technician A is correct because an

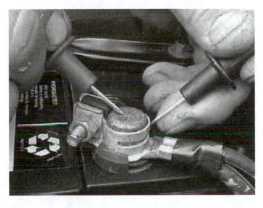

excessive voltage drop (greater than 0.5 volt) can cause the starter to rotate slower than normal during engine cranking. Technician B is correct because resistance anywhere in the power side or ground return side of the cranking of the cranking circuit can cause slow engine cranking. Answers **a, b,** and **d** are not correct because both technicians are correct.

51. **The correct answer is c.** If wires were separated from the commutator of the starter armature, an open circuit would result and little if any current would flow through the starter. Answer **a** (misadjusted starter pinion gear) could cause the starter to drag and draw excessive current if the clearance between the flywheel and the pinion were too close. Answer **b** (loose starter housing) could cause excessive starter current draw if the armature becomes bound due to the misalignment of the armature bushings (bearings). Answer **d** (bent armature) could cause excessive starter current draw when the armature rubs against the field coils when it rotates.

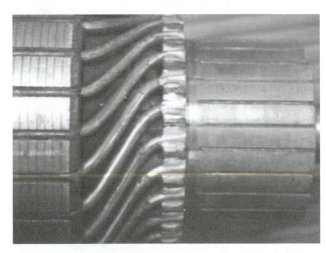

52. **The correct answer is d.** Both answers **a** and **c** are correct. Answer **a** is correct because a bent starter shaft will cause the armature to rub the inside of the field coils (pole shoes) as it rotates during starter motor operation. Answer **c** is correct because worn starter bushings will allow the armature to move away from the center of the starter and rub on the pole shoes. Answer **b** is not correct because a worn commutator, while it could prevent proper starter operation, would not cause the armature to rub on the pole shoes. Answers **a** and **c** are not correct because both **a** and **c** are correct.

53. **The correct answer is c.** Both technicians are correct. Technician A is correct because if the battery cables or connectors have high resistance, the starter solenoid will often click rapidly due to the engagement, releasing, and engagement of the solenoid windings. The solenoid engages when the starter is first being supplied with current, but releases when the starter draw causes the battery voltage to drop low enough to allow the solenoid windings to hold the yoke plunger in the applied position. As soon as the solenoid is released, the battery voltage again is high enough to engage the solenoid and the process repeats. Technician B is correct because if the battery is not at least 75% charged, the results of starter amperage testing may indicate that the starter is defective while the actual cause is a weak battery. Lower than normal battery voltage causes the starter to rotate slower, thereby produces less counter EMF (CEMF) and more current than normal flows from the battery to the starter. Answers **a, b,** and **d** are not correct because both technicians are correct.

54. **The correct answer is a.** A missing solenoid return spring could cause the starter drive to remain engaged in the flywheel after the ignition switch has been released. Answer **b** (starter drive) is not correct because the purpose of the plunger return spring is to force the starter drive out of engagement with the flywheel when the starter stops. Answer **c** is not correct because the most likely result of installing the shift fork backward would be less than full engagement of the drive pinion gear to the flywheel. Answer **d** is not correct because the solenoid contact will operate normally even if installed backward.

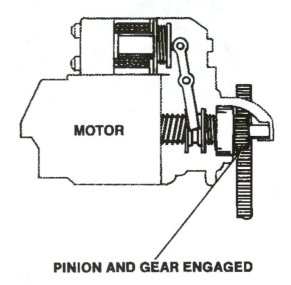

55. **The correct answer is a.** Technician A is correct because a high-scale ammeter is needed to test the current (amperes) draw of a starter. Technician B is not correct because a voltmeter is not required except to measure the battery voltage during the starter test and a high-scale meter is not needed. Answers **c** and **d** are not correct because Technician A only is correct.

56. **The correct answer is d.** Worn starter brushes could affect the operation of the starter but are not as likely to cause a grinding sound. Answer **a** (starter drive) is not correct because a defective drive or pinion gear on the drive could cause a grinding sound. Answer **b** (flywheel) is not correct because if the teeth are excessively worn or damaged, they can cause a grinding sound. Answer **c** (pinion to flywheel clearance) is not correct because if the clearance is not within specifications, a whine or grinding sound could be heard during cranking.

57. **The correct answer is a.** Technician A only is correct because a voltage drop reading of 878 mV (0.878 V) exceeds most vehicle manufacturer's maximum specifications of 0.5 volt (500 mV) and is the result of excessive resistance in the positive cable or at the connection between the cable and the battery terminal. Technician B is not correct because a voltage drop test cannot indicate the condition of a starter motor. Answers **c** and **d** are not correct because Technician A only is correct.

58. **The correct answer is b.** Technician B only is correct because a loose connection will often cause sparks to occur during cranking due to the high current draw of the starter. The loose connection also represents excessive circuit resistance resulting in a starter motor that may not rotate fast enough to start the engine. Technician A is not correct because even though the battery may be discharged or defective, the fact that sparks are observed at the negative cable indicates a connection problem and not necessarily a battery problem. Answers **c** and **d** are not correct because Technician B only is correct.

59. **The correct answer is d.** Neither technician is correct. Technician A is not correct because the voltage should be above 9.6 volts during cranking and the reading of 10.32 exceeds this maximum value. Technician B is not correct because the cranking voltage does not indicate a starter or cranking circuit fault. Answer **c** is not correct because neither technician is correct.

Electrical/Electronic Systems (A6)

D. Charging System Diagnosis and Repair Answers and Explanations

60. **The correct answer is c.** Both technicians are correct. Technician A is correct because if the voltage regulator is defective, no current will flow through the rotor of the generator which is needed to create the magnetic field necessary to create current flow in the stator windings. Technician B is correct because if the brushes are defective, little if any current can flow to the rotor. Answers **a, b,** and **d** are not correct because both technicians are correct.

61. **The correct answer is b.** Technician B only is correct because battery voltage should be measured at the output terminal of the generator (alternator) unless there is an open circuit. The most likely cause of an open circuit between the battery and the generator is a blown fusible link. Technician A is not correct because even though the generator may be defective, the test indicating 0.0 volt at the output terminal is not an indication that it is defective. Answers **c** and **d** are not correct because Technician B only is correct.

62. **The correct answer is a.** The charging system voltage should be within 13.5 to 15.0 volts according to most vehicle manufacturer's specifications. Answer **b** is not correct because 12.6 volts is too low and 15.6 volts is too high and could damage the battery. Answer **c** is not correct because 12 volts is too low a voltage to adequately charge the battery. Answer **d** is not correct because the voltage is too high and could damage the battery and some electrical devices in the vehicle.

63. **The correct answer is c.** Both technicians are correct. Technician A is correct because a good generator should be able to produce at least 13.5 volts. Technician B is correct because a sulfated or defective battery could absorb all of the current produced by the generator and not indicate the proper charging system voltage. Answers **a, b,** and **d** are not correct because both technicians are correct.

64. **The correct answer is a.** Technician A only is correct because to measure a voltage drop between two points of a circuit, current must be flowing. Technician B is not correct because by measuring voltage at the battery terminal, the meter is simply indicating the charging or battery voltage and not the voltage drop of the power side or ground side of the generator circuit. Answers **c** and **d** are not correct because Technician A only is correct.

65. **The correct answer is c.** Both technicians are correct. Technician A is correct because a loose drive belt will slip over the generator drive pulley and not transmit engine power to the generator resulting in reduced or zero generator output. Technician B is correct because a poor ground connection on the case of the generator will create a voltage drop (resistance) in the charging circuit, which will decrease the generator output. Answers **a, b,** and **d** are not correct because both technicians are correct.

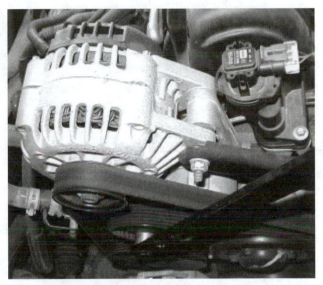

66. **The correct answer is d.** Cold outside temperature is unlikely to cause a generator to produce a lower than specified charging voltage and is likely to cause the voltage to be higher due to the temperature compensation factor built into the electronic voltage regulator or PCM software. Answer **a** (defective battery) is correct because it can cause a lower than normal charging voltage because the battery could be draining all of the output attempting to achieve a full-charge state. Answer **b** is not correct because a low engine speed could reduce the charging voltage. Answer **c** is not correct because a slipping or loose drive belt could decrease the charging voltage, especially at higher engine speeds.

67. **The correct answer is a.** Technician A is correct because a corroded connector between the generator (alternator) and the battery is the likely cause of an excessive voltage drop. Technician B is not correct because a component inside the generator cannot cause a voltage drop in the wiring between the generator (alternator) and the battery. Answers **c** and **d** are not correct because Technician A only is correct.

68. **The correct answer is b.** A defective diode trio will cause a dim charge dash lamp, yet have a limited affect on the output of the generator (alternator). Answers **a** is not correct because a defective rectifier bridge will often not cause the dash warning lamp to light, especially if only one diode out of the six or eight is defective. Answer **c** is not correct because a defective rotor will cause the charge warning lamp to come on bright and not dimly. Answer **d** is not correct because worn brushes will either not cause the warning lamp to come on if they can still supply current to the rotor, or will cause the light to come on with full brightness if the brushes are unable to conduct the necessary current to the rotor through the slip rings.

69. **The correct answer is c.** High resistance in the fusible link between the generator (alternator) and the battery will cause the wire to become hot and will reduce the voltage measured at the battery. Answer **a** is not correct because overcharging is unlikely to cause a lower than normal charging voltage. Answer **b** is not correct because the generator is undercharging as a result of the high voltage drop in the fusible link and is not the cause. Answer **d** is not correct because a poor battery ground could cause a low voltage, but could not cause the fusible link to become hot to the touch.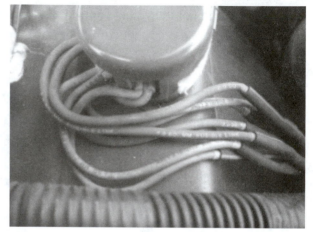

70. **The correct answer is d.** Worn brushes are unlikely to cause a generator to be noisy. Answers **a, b,** and **c** are all possible causes for a noisy generator. Answer **a** (loose drive belt) can cause noise if worn or loose. Answer **b** (defective rectifier diodes) can cause generator noise that is similar to a bearing noise due to the magnetic induction variation that occurs inside a generator if one or more diodes are defective. Answer **c** (defective bearing) will make a growling or rumbling noise.

71. **The correct answer is d.** A diode is an electrical one-way check valve and the meter display should indicate about 0.4 to 0.7 voltage drop when connected in one direction and open circuit (OL) when the meter leads are reversed. Answers **a, b,** and **c** are not correct because they do not indicate the meter reading for a good diode when being tested on the diode check position of a DMM.

Electrical/Electronic Systems (A6)

E. Lighting Systems Diagnosis and Repair Answers and Explanations

72. **The correct answer is d.** It is normal operation on many vehicles because the side marker is wired between the parking light and the turn signal circuits. Opposing voltages would cause the side marker to go out when the lights are on and the turn signal light is on at the same time. Answer **a** is not correct because an open bulb would not light. Answer **b** is not correct because an open turn signal switch would not provide electrical power to cause the turn signals to flash. Answer **c** is not correct because a blown fuse for the parking light circuit would prevent the operation of the parking lamps.

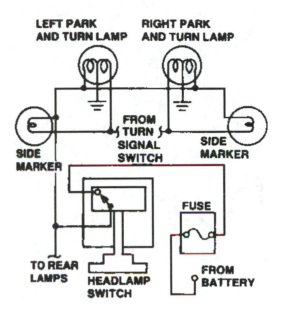

73. **The correct answer is d.** The least likely cause of a dim headlight is a bad sealed beam because it would not light at all. Answers **a**, **b**, and **c** are not correct because all of these are possible explanations that could explain why the right side headlight is dim.

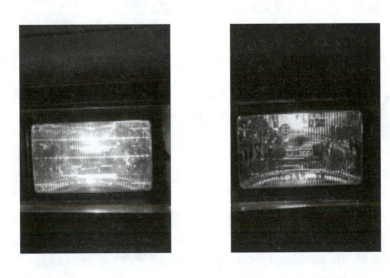

74. **The correct answer is a.** Technician A only is correct because the bulb will not light if it is burned out and yet the high beam will function correctly. Technician B is not correct because the high beam functions correctly, which indicates that the dimmer switch is able to switch to the high beam position. Answers **c** and **d** are not correct because Technician A only is correct.

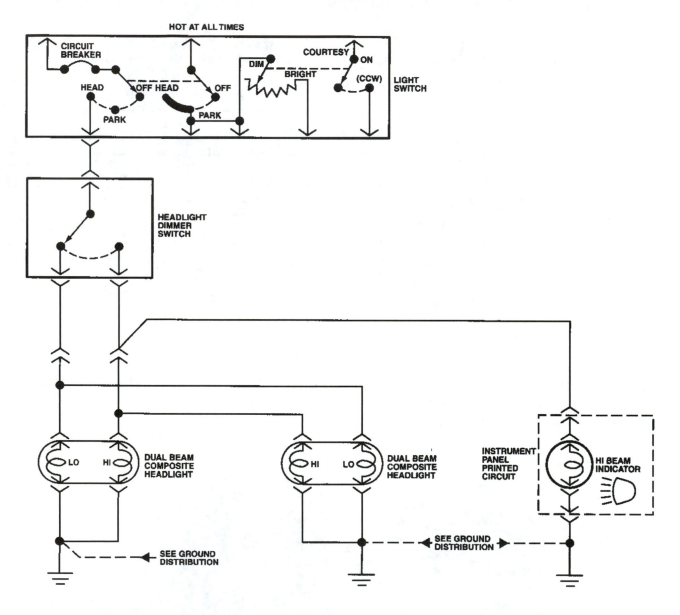

75. **The correct answer is b.** Technician B only is correct because the current flowing through the headlights or parking lights will flow through the turn signal indicator on the dash if the ground connection is corroded or has high resistance. Technician A is not correct because even though it is possible that a short circuit could cause this condition, it is not the most likely. Answers **c** and **d** are not correct because Technician B only is correct.

76. **The correct answer is c.** Halogen bulbs will have a shorter-than-normal service life if bare fingers touch the glass ampoule. The oils from the skin will cause the glass to expand at uneven rates leading to premature failure. Answer **a** is not correct because a poor ground would cause a decrease in electrical current flow through the bulbs, which could affect the operation and brightness but would unlikely decrease the life of the bulbs. Answer **b** is not correct because a shorted headlight switch would not be able to be turned off and while it may cause a battery drain, it would not cause the headlight bulb to have a short service life. Answer **d** is not correct because the bulb cannot be installed backward due to the positioning of the terminals in the electrical connector.

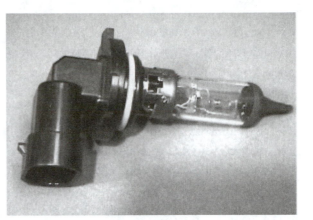

77. **The correct answer is d.** Neither technician is correct. The blown fuse would prevent the operation of the instrument panel lamps. Technician A is not correct because the power for the headlights is entering the headlight switch from the battery and not from the fuse, which is protecting the instrument panel lamp circuit. Technician B is not correct because the electrical power for the taillights and parking lights is entering the headlight switch from the battery and is not affected by the blown fuse for the instrument panel lamp circuit. Answer **c** is not correct because neither technician is correct.

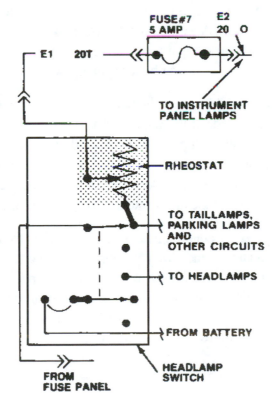

70

78. **The correct answer is a.** Technician A is correct because the current comes from the brake switch through the turn signal switch and to the rear lights. An open in the turn signal switch could prevent the brake lights from working. Technician B is not correct because a defective brake switch, while it could prevent the brake lights from functioning, will not affect the operation of the turn signals. Answers **c** and **d** are not correct because Technician A only is correct.

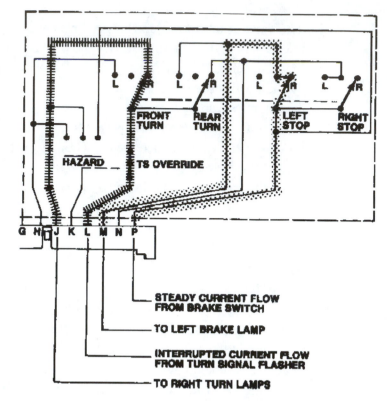

79. **The correct answer is b.** A corroded light socket will cause an increase in circuit resistance causing the bulb to be dimmer than normal due to the reduced current (amperes) flow. Answer **a** is not correct because corrosion causes an increase, not a decrease, in circuit resistance. For a fuse to blow, there has to be a reduction in the circuit resistance, which would increase the current flow above the rating of the fuse. Answer **c** is not correct because even though the additional resistance in the socket could cause a main feedback concern, it is not the most likely cause. Answer **d** is not correct because the lower battery voltage would not cause damage to the bulb.

80. **The correct answer is b.** A defective headlight (open filament) is the most likely cause of the high beam not working on one side of the vehicle. Answer **a** is not correct because a defective dimmer switch would affect both high beam lamps instead of just the right side bulb. Answer **c** is not correct because the ground used for the high beam is the same ground used for the low beam and the low beam is functioning correctly. Answer **d** is not correct because a discharged battery would affect the operation of all of the lights and not just the right-side high beam.

81. **The correct answer is a.** A misadjusted neutral safety switch is the most likely cause of the backup lights remaining on all the time. Most neutral safety switches contain contacts that close when the gear selector is in reverse to send current to the backup (reverse) lights. Answer **b** is not correct because an open switch means that no current will flow through the switch. Answers **c** and **d** are not correct because even if the bulb were installed backward, the lights would not remain on because the power comes from the neutral safety switch.

82. **The correct answer is a.** A poor ground will cause the light to go out when additional current is applied because the connection will become hot, increasing the resistance even higher, which will reduce the current flow through the bulb enough that it appears to go out completely. Answer **b** is not correct because a shorted bulb would not light at all. Answer **c** is not correct because a defective brake switch would affect both rear brake lights and since the right brake light functions correctly, the fault has to be somewhere else. Answer **d** is not correct because the bulb lights are OK.

83. **The correct answer is b.** Technician B only is correct because when trailer lights are connected, more current than normal flows through the flasher, creating the rapid flashing indicating a fault to the driver. The technician should replace the flasher unit or rewire the trailer lights using a relay to avoid this problem. Technician A is not correct because even if the wiring were reversed, additional current will flow through the turn signal flasher and create the rapid flashing. Answers **c** and **d** are not correct because Technician B only is correct.

84. **The correct answers is d.** All of the above could result. Answer **a** is correct because the ground for the side marker light often flows through the front turn signal bulb and without this ground, the current would flow through and light the turn signal indicator lamp on the dash. Answer **b** is correct because a defective (shorted) brake light will create a path from the brake light circuit to the taillight circuit, which can then allow current to flow to the dash lights when the brake pedal is depressed. Answer **c** is correct because if the brake light bulb was shorted to the taillight circuit, the electronics may be activated indicating that the lights are on even though they are off but the brake pedal has been depressed with the ignition key off.

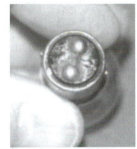

85. **The correct answer is d.** All of the above are correct. Answer **a** is correct because a defective brake switch will prevent cruise control operation. Answer **b** is correct because the brake pedal switch is an input to many ABS units and uses this signal to get ready to handle a possible ABS event. Without the brake pedal input, the application of the ABS operation could be delayed and/or set an ABS related diagnostic trouble code (DTC). Answer **c** is correct because the shifter will not be able to be moved from the park position if the shift solenoid does not receive voltage from the brake switch.

86. **The correct answer is c.** Both technicians are correct. Technician A is correct because a higher wattage bulb will draw more current than the standard bulb. This extra current and bulb wattage can overheat the bulb socket and burn the insulation of the wiring as well as damage the headlight and dimmer switch. Technician B is correct because adding extra lighting in parallel with the existing lights increases the current flow through the headlight and dimmer switches. Answers **a**, **b**, and **d** are not correct because both technicians are correct.

Electrical/Electronic Systems (A6)

F. Gauges, Warning Devices, and Driver Information Systems
Diagnosis and Repair Answers and Explanations

87. **The correct answer is c.** Both technicians are correct. Technician A is correct because a corroded connector will increase the resistance in the circuit and affect the accuracy of the fuel level gauge. Technician B is correct because if the electrical connector were disconnected, the fuel level gauge will read high or low depending on the design of the circuit because the resistance becomes infinity when unplugged. Answers **a, b,** and **d** are not correct because both technicians are correct.

88. **The correct answer is a.** Technician A only is correct because the pressure differential switch will provide the electrical ground for the red brake warning lamp if there is a difference in pressure between the two separate brake systems. When the wire was removed, the dash light went out indicating that it was in fact the pressure differential switch that was grounding the light circuit. Technician B is not correct because if the parking brake had been applied (or the switch was stuck), the red brake warning lamp would not have gone out when the wire was removed from the pressure differential switch. Answers **c** and **d** are not correct because Technician A only is correct.

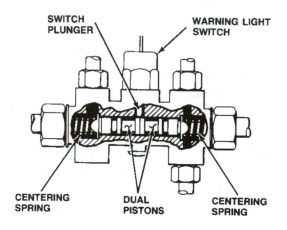

89. **The correct answer is b.** A burned out bulb is the most likely cause for the charge indicator lamp to not light when the ignition is on (run) and the engine is off. Answer **a** is not correct because even though a blown fusible link will cause a no charge condition, it is not likely to prevent the dash warning lamp from lighting when the ignition is on and the engine is off. Answers **c** and **d** are not correct because even though a defective diode (answer **c**) or a short inside the generator (answer **d**) could cause a no charging condition, they are unlikely to cause the red dash warning lamp to not light when the ignition is on and the engine is off.

90. **The correct answer is b.** A defective bulb is the most likely cause for the turn signals to not flash on one side. If both front and rear bulbs do not work, the current flow through the flasher unit is not enough to heat the bimetallic strip inside, which would then open the circuit, cool, and make contact again. Answer **a** (defective flasher) is not correct because the right side functions okay and the same flasher unit is used for both sides. Answer **c** is not likely to cause the turn signals to not flash

91.   on one side only. Answer **d** (low battery voltage) is not likely to prevent the turn signals from flashing on one side only.

92. **The correct answer is c.** Both technicians are correct. Technician A is correct because the movement of the dash gauge, when the sending unit wire was grounded, indicated that the gauge will react to changes in resistance in the circuit. Technician B is correct because the test checked that the wiring and the dash unit were able to function and react to changes in resistance in the circuit, which leaves just the tank sending unit as the most likely cause for the inoperative fuel gauge. Answers **a, b,** and **d** are not correct because both technicians are correct.

93. **The correct answer is a.** The most likely cause of the oil pressure warning lamp to be on all the time, even though the oil pressure is normal, is a defective oil pressure sending unit. Most sending units provide the ground for the warning lamp circuit and if the sending unit was shorted, the lamp would light whenever the ignition was on. Answer **b** is not correct because a shorted dash warning lamp would not light at all and therefore could not be the cause. Answer **c** is not correct because an open wire would prevent the sending unit from providing the ground necessary to complete the circuit for the warning lamp. Answer **d** is not correct because the oil pressure was measured to be OK and the problem is in the light circuit not with the engine.

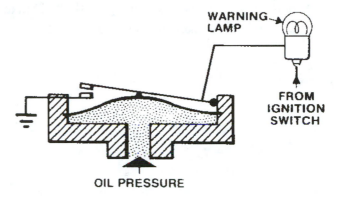

94. **The correct answer is a.** Technician A only is correct because the larger diameter tire will travel farther with each revolution, but the odometer will simply record the mileage as if the stock wheels and tires were on the vehicle. The amount of fuel is divided into the miles traveled so the calculated fuel economy will be lower than actual. Technician B is not correct because the new tires will rotate slower at any given speed and will, therefore, indicate a speed slower than the actual speed. Answers **c** and **d** are not correct because Technician A only is correct.

95. **The correct answer is d.** Having too much antifreeze in the coolant is not likely to affect the coolant temperature of the engine. Answers **a, b,** and **c** are possible causes for a coolant temperature gauge to register cold all the time.

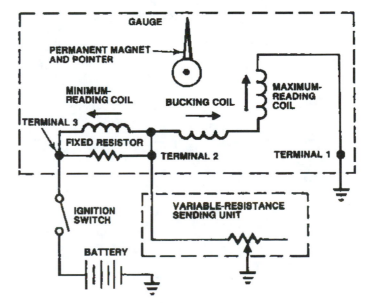

96. **The correct answer is c.** A burned out bulb on the left side is the most likely cause of a rapid turn indicator lamp blinking on one side only. The flasher unit causes the dash turn indicator lamp to blink rapidly to warn the driver that there is a fault in the system as a safety measure required of all vehicle manufacturers. Some vehicles will cause the turn indicator lamp to not flash at all if there is a fault. Answer **a** is not correct because a defective flasher unit would affect both sides and not just the left side turn signals. Answer **b** is not correct because the turn signals work as designed on the right side indicating that all of the bulbs on the right are functioning. Answer **d** is not correct because even though a shorted brake switch could cause the brake light to be on all the time, it is unlikely to cause a fault with only the left side turn signals.

Electrical/Electronic Systems (A6)

G. Horn and Wiper/Washer Diagnosis and Repair
Answers and Explanations

96. **The correct answer is c.** The adjusting screw on a horn, if there is one, adjusts the clarity (tone) of the horn. The usual procedure is to operate the horn with an ammeter connected in series and adjust the screw until the amperage reading is within factory specifications for the model being tested. Answers **a, b,** and **d** are not

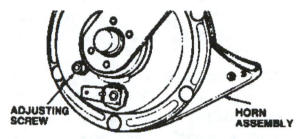

correct because the adjustment changes the tone and not the frequency or the volume. The voltage is supplied from the battery and not from the horn.

97. **The correct answer is a.** Technician A is correct because a poor electrical ground connection can prevent one horn from operating, yet not affect the other horn because each horn is mounted separately to the body or frame of the vehicle. Technician B is not correct because a defect in the horn contact ring would affect both horns. Answers **c** and **d** are not correct because Technician A only is correct.

98. **The correct answer is a.** Technician A is correct because the relay coil measures 70 ohms right in the middle of the usual reading of between 50 and 100 ohms for most relay coils. The OL reading between terminals #2 and #4 indicates that the relay contacts are open, which they should be until the coil is energized. Technician B is not correct because it is normal for the contacts to be open when the coil of the relay is not energized. Answers **c** and **d** are not correct because Technician A only is correct.

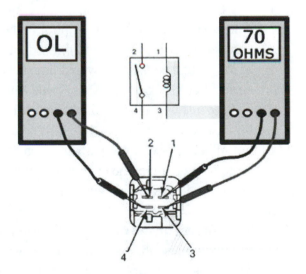

99. **The correct answer is c.** Both technicians are correct. Technician A is correct because a defective horn will often sound garbled or not produce a clear tone, especially if water has gotten into the horn and has frozen. Technician B is correct because most horns are grounded through the mounting bolt and if this bolt were loose, a poor ground would result causing a decrease in current flow through the horn. Answers **a, b,** and **d** are not correct because both technicians are correct.

100.   **The correct answer is b.** Most horn switches operate by grounding the circuit for the horn relay. If this switch were to fail and become grounded all the time, the horn would blow all the time. Answer **a** is not correct because an open in the horn relay would break the flow of current to the horns and not cause it to be energized all the time. Answer **c** is not correct because a poor ground would cause an increase in circuit resistance and a decrease in current flow through the horn causing the horn to sound fainter than normal and could not cause it to blow all the time. Answer **d** is not correct because a defective horn would not function or function poorly and could not be the cause of blowing all the time.

101.   **The correct answer is a.** A shorted horn wire is the least likely cause of an inoperative horn because this fault would not cause the relay to click. Answer **b** is not correct because if the relay contacts were corroded, the resistance created would prevent enough current to operate the horn, yet the contacts will still move and click as the relay coil is energized. Answer **c** is

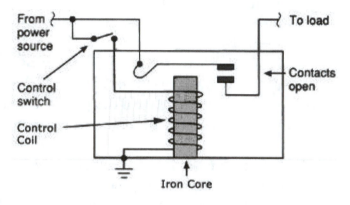

not correct because a defective horn could allow the relay to click but not sound because of a fault within the horn itself. Answer **d** is not correct because an open horn ground connection would prevent the horn from working, yet the relay would still click when energized.

102.   **The correct answer is d.** A poor body-to-engine ground can cause problems with any accessory that is grounded to the body if more than one unit is operating because the resistance of the ground connection would limit the total current flow through the devices. Answer **a** is not correct because worn brushes would cause the wiper motor to not operate correctly at all times and not just when the headlights or the blower motor is operating. Answer **b** is not correct because a weak battery, while it could cause the wipers to operate slower than normal, is not the most likely cause of this particular condition. Answer **c** is not correct because a defective wiper switch would affect the operation of the wipers at all times and not just when the blower motor or the headlights are in operation.

103.   **The correct answer is a.** Technician A is correct because most two-speed motors use several windings or use three brushes to achieve the two wiper motor speeds. If the wiper motor itself has a fault in one of the brushes or windings, the motor is likely to operate on only one speed. Technician B is not correct because a poor ground would cause wiper problems on both speeds, not just one speed. Answers **c** and **d** are not correct because Technician A only is correct.

104. **The correct answer is b.** Technician B is correct because the park mechanism is incorporated into the wiper motor assembly. Even though some wipers can be repaired for this fault, in most cases the entire wiper motor assembly must be replaced. Technician A is not correct because a poor ground for the wiper circuit would cause the wiper motor to operate slower than normal and is unlikely to cause the wipers to fail to park properly. Answers **c** and **d** are not correct because Technician B only is correct.

105. **The correct answer is c.** Both technicians are correct. Technician A is correct because a blown fusible link could prevent electrical power from reaching the blower motor. Technician B says that a defective engine fan relay could prevent power from reaching the fan motor. Answers **a, b,** and **d** are not correct because both technicians are correct.

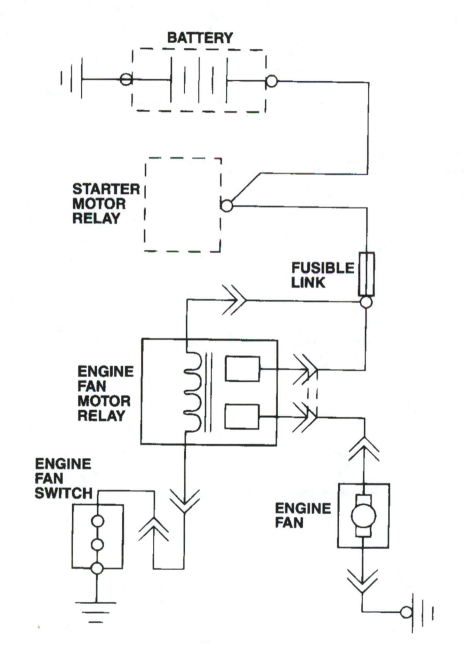

106. **The correct answer is d.** If an open occurred at the relay, the current could not flow from the fuse 18 through the intermittent relay and to the low speed brush on the wiper motor. Answer **a** is not correct because terminal #28 affects the operation of the low speed, not the high speed because the high-speed brush is off to the side creating a lower resistance path to ground causing more current to flow resulting in a faster rotating motor. Answer **b** is not correct because the wiper will function correctly on low speed through terminal #11 at the relay. Answer **c** is not

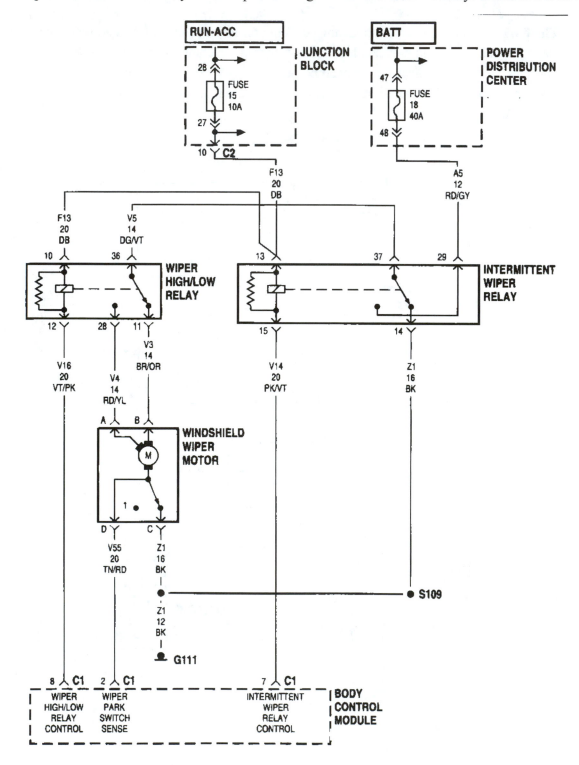

Electrical/Electronic Systems (A6)

H. Accessories Diagnosis and Repair Answers and Explanations

107. **The correct answer is c.** The least likely cause of a radio not receiving AM, but receiving FM signals would be high resistance in the radio power feed wire. Answer **a** is not correct because a defective antenna will allow FM reception, yet not AM. Answer **b** is not correct because a fault inside the radio with the AM tuner could cause the problem. Answer **d** is not correct because a poor antenna ground will allow FM but often no AM reception.

108. **The correct answer is b.** The wiring and connectors for airbags are usually yellow to help identify them. Answers **a, c,** and **d** are not correct because most airbag connectors are yellow.

109. **The correct answer is c.** Both technicians are correct. Technician A is correct because even though the blower motor operates, it may be drawing more than the specified current. A fused jumper lead equipped with a 20 A fuse is a commonly used method to determine if the motor is drawing more than 20 A. Technician B is correct because an open in the fan control relay or resistor pack could cause the blower motor to not operate. Answers **a, b,** and **d** are not correct because both technicians are correct.

110. **The correct answer is d.** Neither technician is correct. Technician A is not correct because corroded ground connections would cause an increase in circuit resistance and a decrease (rather than an increase) in current flow through the motor. Technician B is not correct because a shorted blower relay would cause the blower motor to run all the time and would not cause the motor to draw more current as would occur if the motor itself were defective. Answer **c** is not correct because neither technician is correct.

111. **The correct answer is a.** Technician A is correct because if the power is lost to the independent door switch, it cannot operate the window either up or down. The master control switch is still able to function normally even if the independent door switch has lost its power lead by supplying power and ground to the window motor. Technician B is not correct because without power, the independent switch cannot supply power to operate the window in either direction. Answers **c** and **d** are not correct because Technician A only is correct.

112. **The correct answer is a.** Technician A is correct because an open high pressure cutout switch would prevent the operation of the A/C compressor clutch. Technician B is not correct because the diode is used to reduce the voltage spike that occurs when the clutch is disengaged and would not prevent the clutch from engaging. Answers **c** and **d** are not correct because Technician A only is correct.

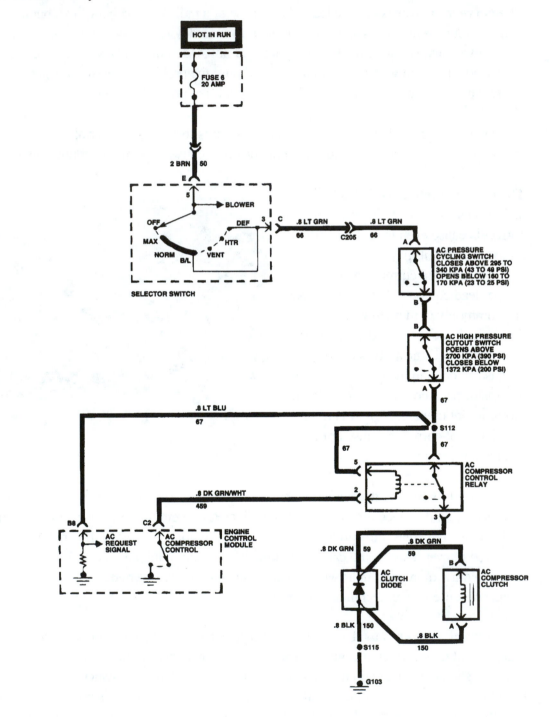

113. **The correct answer is a.** Technician A is correct because a bumpy road could cause the brake safety switch to open the circuit to the cruise control. The safety switch is normally used to disable the cruise control when the driver applies the brakes. Technician B is not correct because even though care should be exercised when driving over bumpy roads, it is not normal for the cruise control to be disabled under these conditions. Answers **c** and **d** are not correct because Technician A only is correct.

114. **The correct answer is b.** A binding headlight door would cause the electric motor to operate at a slower speed and therefore produce less counter EMF and draw more current from the vehicle battery than normal. Answer **a** is not correct because a bad ground would increase circuit resistance thereby reducing current flow. Answer **c** is not correct because a loose connection would create heat and a voltage drop resulting in increased circuit resistance and a decrease, rather than an increase, in current flow to the motor. Answer **d** is not correct because a blown fuse would create an open circuit stopping the flow of current through the motor.

115. **The correct answer is b.** Worn or dry bearings will cause the motor to drag and operate at a slower than normal speed. Answer **a** is not correct because a blown resistor would cause an open circuit and prevent blower motor operation. Answer **c** is not correct because a bad switch could create a high resistance in the circuit but would more likely fail open, thereby stopping the operation of the blower motor. Answer **d** is not correct because an open switch will stop the flow of electrical power to the motor and the motor would not operate.

116. **The correct answer is c.** Both technicians are correct. Technician A is correct because if the antenna is loose or has a poor ground connection, the signal will be weak leading to static and poor reception. Technician B is correct because a poor ground on the radio chassis itself can lead to sound quality problems. Answers **a, b,** and **d** are not correct because both technicians are correct.

117. **The correct answer is b.** If all of the power locks but one operate correctly, the most likely cause is a defective power door lock solenoid or motor. Answer **a** is not correct because a poor connection at the power door lock relay would cause problems with all, not just one, of the power door locks. Answer **c** is not correct because an open circuit breaker would prevent the operation of all of the power door locks. Answer **d** is not correct because an open (blown) fuse would create an open circuit and no electrical power would be available to any of the power door locks, not just one.

118. **The correct answer is d.** The most likely cause for a speaker to not function is the speaker itself being defective. Answer **a** is not correct because a defective audio unit, while it could affect just one speaker if defective, is likely to cause problems with more than one speaker. Answer **b** is not correct because a poor ground at G502 would affect all speakers the same and not just the left rear. Answer **c** is not correct because an open antenna lead would affect the radio reception and affect all speakers the same and not just the left rear.

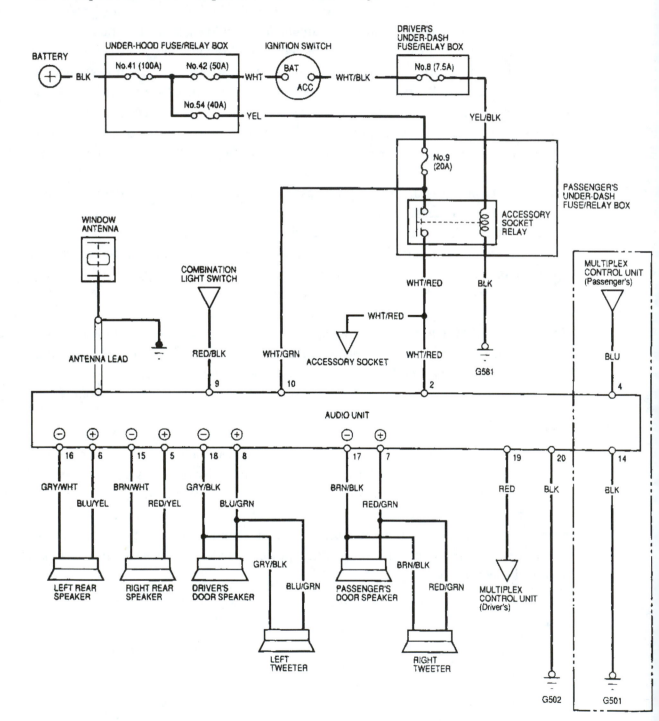

119. **The correct answer is a.** Technician A is correct because many devices are operated directly by an electronic module from inputs from switches. If a scan tool can operate the trunk release, then this test confirms that the module and the trunk release solenoid circuits are functional. If the scan tool cannot operate the trunk, then the technician knows that the problem could be the trunk release circuit, switches, or the control module. Technician B is not correct because even though the dash switch could be defective, it is unlikely to cause the trunk release to not function from either the switch or the remote. Answers **c** and **d** are not correct because Technician A only is correct.

120. **The correct answer is d.** Neither technician is correct. Technician A is not correct because an open thermal limiter would prevent the fan motor from operating at any speed, except high, and could not be the cause of the fan operating at low speed only. Technician B is not correct because an open at the "LO" contact in the switch would not affect the operation of the fan on the LO setting because no current flows through the switch when the low position is selected. Answers **a, b,** and **c** are not correct because neither technician is correct.

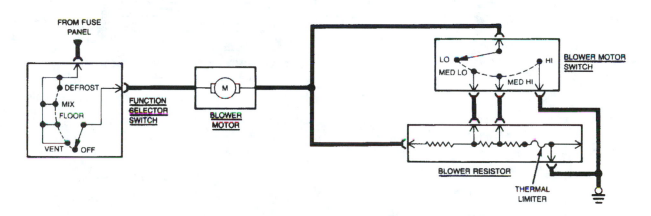

121. **The correct answer is b.** The voltage should drop as current flows through the rear window defogger grids due to the resistance of the heater wires. The power side of the grid should measure about 12 volts as shown and zero volts at the ground side. At the midpoint, the voltmeter should measure about 6 volts. Answers **a, c,** and **d** are not correct because these answers do not state the correct voltage at the midpoint.

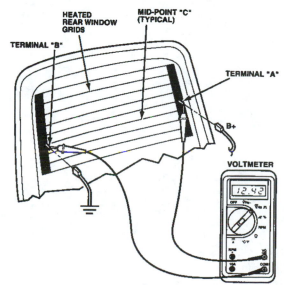

122. **The correct answer is d.** Neither technician is correct. Technician A is not correct because the indicator light is a separate section of the circuit connected in parallel and the bulb burning out would not affect the operation of the rear window defogger. Technician B is not correct because the light bulb does not affect the operation of the relay or the rear window defogger except that the driver will not see the indicator light come on when the defogger is turned on.

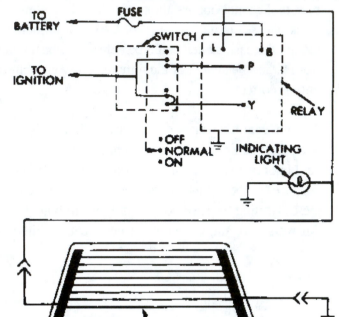

Electrical/Electronic Systems (A6)

Appendix 1 – Environmental Questions

All automotive service operations assume that the service technician will adhere to proper handling and disposal of all automotive waste. Questions about environmental issues are not asked on the actual ASE test, but these sample questions will test your knowledge of the proper ways to handle these issues.

1. Hazardous materials include all of the following except _____.

    a. Engine oil
    b. Asbestos
    c. Water
    d. Brake cleaner

2. To determine if a product or substance being used is hazardous, consult _____.

    a. A dictionary
    b. A MSDS
    c. SAE standards
    d. EPA guidelines

3. Technician A says that used engine oil can be used in waste oil heaters. Technician B says that waste oil can be recycled by a licensed recycler. Which technician is correct?

    a. Technician A only
    b. Technician B only
    c. Both Technicians A and B
    d. Neither Technician A nor B

4. Two technicians are discussing what to do with used antifreeze coolant. Technician A says that it can be recycled either onsite or offsite. Technician B says that it can be poured down the drain. Which technician is correct?

    a. Technician A only
    b. Technician B only
    c. Both Technicians A and B
    d. Neither Technician A nor B

5. Used antifreeze coolant is often considered hazardous waste because it contains _____.

    a. Ethyl glycol
    b. Water (H_2O)
    c. Dissolved metal(s)
    d. Organic acids

6. Two technicians are discussing corrosive materials. Technician A says that a substance with a pH of 2 or lower is a strong acid. Technician B says that a substance with a pH of 12.5 or higher is caustic. Which technician is correct?

    a. Technician A only
    b. Technician B only
    c. Both Technicians A and B
    d. Neither Technician A nor B

7. Two technicians are discussing material safety data sheets (MSDS). Technician A says to look for the ingredients that contain the letters "clor" or "fluor". Technician B says to look for a flash point below 140°F (60°C). Which technician is correct?

    a. Technician A only
    b. Technician B only
    c. Both Technicians A and B
    d. Neither Technician A nor B

8. Two technicians are discussing used batteries. Technician A says that they should be considered hazardous waste and should be recycled by a licensed recycler. Technician B says to store used batteries near a drain in case they leak acid. Which technician is correct?

    a. Technician A only
    b. Technician B only
    c. Both Technicians A and B
    d. Neither Technician A nor B

9. Technician A says that gasoline should always be stored in red containers. Technician B says that gasoline should always be stored in sealed containers. Which technician is correct?

    a. Technician A only
    b. Technician B only
    c. Both Technicians A and B
    d. Neither Technician A nor B

10. Hazardous waste should be handled by the shop or repair facility and records kept of which of the following:

    a. Name of the company or individual that disposes of the waste
    b. Where it is being sent
    c. What is going to happen to the waste
    d. All of the above

Electrical/Electronic Systems (A6)

Appendix 1 – Environmental Answers

1. **The correct answer is c.** Water is not considered to be a hazardous material unless it is contaminated by other elements that are considered to be hazardous. Answer **c** is not correct because engine oil is considered to be hazardous because of the dissolved metals and accumulated acid that used oil contains. Answer **b** is not correct because asbestos is considered to be a cancer causing material if breathed. Answer **d** is not correct because brake cleaner often contains solvents or other volatile organic compounds (VOL) that are considered to be hazardous.

2. **The correct answer is b.** The material safety data sheet (MSDS) is the best source for information regarding a product or substance. Answer **a** is not correct because a product or substance is often a combination of ingredients and would not be listed or described in a dictionary. Answers **c** and **d** are not correct because even though these organizations have established standards, the product or substance could meet these standards and still be considered hazardous.

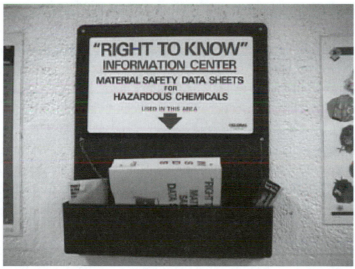

3. **The correct answer is c.** Technician A is correct because waste oil can be burned in a waste oil heater with a capacity of less than 500,000 BTUs. Technician B is correct because used (waste) oil can be recycled by a licensed recycler. Answers **a**, **b**, and **d** are not correct because both technicians are correct.

4. **The correct answer is a.** Used antifreeze coolant can be recycled either on site or shipped to a licensed recycler off site. Technician B is not correct because unless a permit is applied for and granted, it is generally not acceptable to pour used coolant down a sanitary sewer. Answers **c** and **d** are not correct because only Technician A is correct.

5. **The correct answer is c.** Antifreeze coolant (ethylene glycol) by itself is not considered to be hazardous. When the coolant is used in an engine, it can absorb metals such as iron, steel, copper, and lead from the cooling system components, which can cause the coolant to become hazardous. Answer **a** is not correct because most coolant is mostly ethylene glycol with about 5% additives and by itself is not considered to be hazardous. Answer **b** is not correct because even though water containing chemicals can be considered to be hazardous, water by itself is not hazardous. Answer **d** is not correct because the acid content would have to be high enough to lower the pH form about 7-12 down to 2 or less to be considered hazardous.

6. **The correct answer is c.** Technician A is correct because a pH of 2 or less is considered to be strong acid and is very corrosive. Technician B is correct because any substance with a pH of 12.5 or higher is very caustic and is considered to be hazardous. Answers **a**, **b**, and **d** are not correct because both technicians are correct.

7. **The correct answer is c.** Technician A is correct because most hazardous materials contain chemicals that have the letter "clor" or "fluor" in their ingredients as described in the material safety data sheet (MSDS). Technician B is correct because a material is considered to be hazardous if it has a flash point (temperature where it will ignite) below 140°F (60°C). Gasoline is an example of a product that has a flash temperature below 140°F. Answers **a**, **b**, and **d** are not correct because both technicians are correct.

8. **The correct answer is a.** Used batteries should be recycled and transported to an EPA approved recycling facility. Answer **b** is not correct because batteries should be stored away from drains to prevent the possibility that battery acid could seep into the sanitary or storm sewer. Answers **c** and **d** are not correct because only Technician A is correct.

9. **The correct answer is c.** Technician A is correct because gasoline should only be stored in red containers for easy identification. Technician B is correct because gasoline should always be stored in a sealed container to prevent the escape of gasoline fumes, which could be easily ignited. Answers **a**, **b**, and **d** are not correct because both technicians are correct.

10. **The correct answer is d.** A shop handling hazardous waste must keep records which include **a** the name of the company or individual that disposes of the waste, **b** the location where the material is sent, and **c** how the waste is going to be disposed of when it reaches the site. Answers **a**, **b**, and **c** are not correct because all three answers are correct.

Electrical/Electronic Systems (A6)

Appendix 2 – Safety Questions

All automotive service operations assume that the service technician will practice safe work habits. Questions about safety issues are not asked on the actual ASE test, but these sample questions will test your knowledge of the proper ways to handle these issues.

1. All equipment used in the shop must be designed to meet what safety standards?

   a. Occupational Safety and Health Act (OSHA)
   b. Environmental Protection Agency (EPA)
   c. Resource Conservation and Recovery Act (RCRA)
   d. Workplace Hazardous Material Information Systems (WHMIS)

2. All items are considered to be personal protection equipment (PPE) **except**:

   a. Safety glasses
   b. Gloves
   c. Hearing protection
   d. Hair net

3. When should service technicians wear ear protection?

   a. If the sound level is high enough that you must raise your voice to be heard
   b. Above 90 dB (a lawnmower is about 110 dB)
   c. When using a torch
   d. Both a and b

4. A service technician should _____.

   a. Pull on a wrench
   b. Push on a wrench
   c. Use your legs when lifting heavy loads
   d. Both a and c

5. A three-prong 110-volt plug is being used, but it will not fit the two-prong outlet. What should the technician do?

   a. Cut off the round ground prong
   b. Use an adapter from the three-prong plug to the two-prong electrical outlet
   c. Attach a grounded adapter and connect the green ground wire to the outlet housing before using the electrical device
   d. Use a cordless tool

6. Personal protection equipment (PPE) can include _____.

    a. Steel-toe shoes
    b. Face mask
    c. Gloves
    d. All of the above

7. The shop should have _____.

    a. Guards in good condition installed on machinery
    b. Shop/bay floors that are clean and dry
    c. Fire extinguishers that are properly charged and easily accessible
    d. All of the above

8. What type of fire extinguisher should be used to put out an oil or grease fire?

    a. Water
    b. CO_2
    c. Dry chemical
    d. Either b or c

9. To what does the term "lockout" or LO/TO refer?

    a. A union strike
    b. A lock placed on the lever that disconnects electrical power
    c. A type of hand tool
    d. A safety ground fault switch

10. A service technician should wear personal protection equipment to be protected against all **except** _____.

    a. Used oil
    b. Pumice-type cleaners
    c. Falling heavy objects
    d. Loud noises

Electrical/Electronic Systems (A6)

Appendix 2 – Safety Question Answers

1. **The correct answer is a.** Shop equipment must meet the standards established by the Occupational Safety and Health Act (OSHA). Answers **b**, **c**, and **d** are not correct because the EPA, RCRA, and WHMIS regulate air, water, ground contamination, and hazardous materials and are not associated with the specifications of shop equipment.

2. **The correct answer is d.** Answer **d** is correct; a hair net is used to prevent hair from falling into food and is not generally considered to be safety equipment, even though long hair could get caught in machinery. Answers **a**, **b**, and **c** are all considered to be personal protection equipment.

3. **The correct answer is d.** Answer **a** is correct because ear protection should be worn if the surrounding noise level is high enough that it requires you to raise your voice to be heard. Answer **b** is correct because the OSHA standard requires that ear protection be used whenever noise levels exceed 90 dB. Answer **c** is not correct because a torch will usually not create noise above 90 dB.

4. **The correct answer is d.** Answer **a** is correct because a technician should pull (instead of push) a wrench. Answer **c** is correct because a technician should use his/her legs and not his/her back to lift heavy objects. Answer **b** is not correct because a technician could be injured by pushing on a wrench when the fastener breaks loose or if the wrench slips.

5. **The correct answer is c.** Answer **c** is correct because a three-prong plug to a two-prong electrical outlet adapter has a green wire pigtail that should be attached to the outlet box to be assured that the device is properly grounded. Answer **a** is not correct because if the ground prong is cut off, the device has no electrical path to ground and could create a shock hazard. Answer **b** is not correct because simply using an adapter without grounding the adapter prevents the device from being properly grounded, which could cause a shock hazard. Answer **d** is not correct because even though a cordless tool would not create a hazard, the question states that a three-prong plug is being used and the best answer is **c**.

6. **The correct answer is d.** Answers **a**, **b**, and **c** are correct because steel-toe shoes, face mask, and gloves are all considered to be personal protection equipment (PPE). Answers **a**, **b**, and **c** are not correct because all three items are considered to be PPE, not just one of the items.

7. **The correct answer is d.** Answer **a** is correct because guards must be installed on all machinery that requires a guard and they must be in good condition. Answer **b** is correct because the shop/bay floors should be clean and dry to prevent slippage, which could cause personal injury. Answer **c** is correct because fire extinguishers must be fully charged and easily accessible. Answers **a**, **b**, and **c** are not correct because all three items should be present in all shops.

8. **The correct answer is d.** Answer **b** is correct because a CO_2 fire extinguisher can be used on almost any type of fire including an oil or grease fire. Answer **c** is correct because a dry chemical fire extinguisher can also be used on most types of fires including an oil and grease fire. Answer **a** is not correct because water is heavier than oil and will cause the oil to float on the surface of the water.

9. **The correct answer is b.** Answer **b** is correct because the term lock out/try out (LO/TO) refers to physically installing a lock on the electrical box that would prevent the accidental switching on of electrical power to the circuit being serviced. Answer **a** is not correct because even though the term lockout is used to describe some actions, the term LO/TO is used mostly to describe the locking out of an electrical circuit. Answers **c** and **d** are not correct because they do not describe the locking out of electrical power.

10. **The correct answer is b.** Answer **b** is correct because pumice-type cleaners are typically used to wash hands and are not considered to be hazardous. Answers **a**, **c**, and **d** are not correct because the question asks which is not a possible hazardous material.

A6 English-Language Glossary

Alternator - An electric generator that produces alternating current.

AM - Amplitude modulation.

Ammeter - An electrical test instrument used to measure amperes (unit of the amount of current flow). An ammeter is connected in series with the circuit being tested.

Ampere - The unit of the amount of current flow. Named for André Ampère (1775–1836).

Ampere turns - The unit of measurement for electrical magnetic field strength.

Analog - A type of dash instrument that indicates values by use of the movement of a needle or similar device. An analog signal is continuous and variable.

Anode - The positive electrode; the electrode toward which electrons flow.

Antimony - A metal added to nonmaintenance-free or hybrid battery grids to add strength.

Armature - The rotating unit inside a DC generator or starter, consisting of a series of coils of insulating wire wound around a laminated iron core.

Atom - The smallest unit of matter that still retains separate unique characteristics of each element.

AWG - American wire gauge system.

Bakelite - A brand name of the Union Carbide Company for phenolformaldehyde resin plastic.

Base - The name for the section of a transistor that controls the current flow through the transistor.

Battery - A chemical device that produces a voltage created by two dissimilar metals submerged in an electrolyte.

Bendix drive - An inertia-type starter engagement mechanism not used on vehicles since the early 1960s.

Bias - In electrical terms, the voltage applied to a device or component to establish the reference point for operation.

Blower motor - An electric motor and squirrel cage type of fan moving air inside the vehicle for heating, cooling, and defrosting.

BNC connector - A type of connector used on digital and analog scopes. Named for its inventor, Baby Neil Councilman.

Brushes - A copper or carbon conductor used to transfer electrical current from or to a revolving electrical part such as that used in an electric motor or generator.

Burn in - A process of operating an electronic device for a period from several hours to several days.

Calcium - A metallic chemical element added to the grids of a maintenance-free battery to add strength.

Candlepower - The amount of light produced by a bulb.

Capacitance - Electrical capacitance is a term used to measure or describe how much charge can be stored in a capacitor (condenser) for a given voltage potential difference. Capacitance is measured in farads or smaller increments of farads, such as microfarads.

Capacitor - A condenser; an electrical unit that can pass alternating current, yet block direct current. Used in electrical circuits to control fluctuations in voltage.

Carbon pile - An electrical test instrument used to provide an electrical load for testing batteries and the charging circuit.

Cathode - The negative electrode.

Cell - A group of negative and positive plates assembled to form a unit capable of producing 2.1 V. Each cell contains one more negative plate than positive plate.

CEMF - Counter electromotive force.

Charging circuit - Electrical components and connections necessary to keep a battery fully charged. Components include the alternator, voltage regulator, battery, and interconnecting wires.

Chassis ground - In electrical terms, a ground is the desirable return circuit path. Ground can also be undesirable and provide a shortcut path for a defective electrical circuit.

Circuit - The path that electrons travel from a power source, through a resistance, and back to the power source.

Circuit breaker - A mechanical unit that opens an electrical circuit in the event of excessive flow.

Cold cranking amperes - (CCA) The rating of a battery's ability to provide battery voltage during cold-weather operation. CCA is the number of amperes that a battery can supply at 0°F (-18°C) for 30 seconds and still maintain a voltage of 1.2 V per cell (7.2 V for a 12-V battery).

Collector - The name of one section of a transistor.

Commutator - The name for the copper segments of the armature of a starter or DC generator. The revolving segments of the commutator collect the current from or distribute it to the brushes.

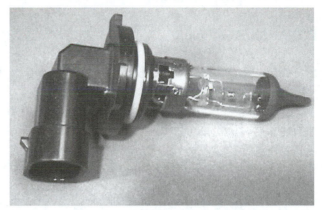

Composite headlights - A type of headlight that uses a separate replaceable bulb.

Compound wound - A type of electric motor where some field coils are wired in series and some field coils are wired in parallel with the armature.

Conductor - A material that conducts electricity and heat. A metal that contains fewer than four electrons in its atom's outer shell.

Conventional theory - The theory that electricity flows from positive (+) to negative (-).

Courtesy light - General term used to describe all interior lights.

Cranking circuit - Electrical components and connections required to crank the engine to start. Includes starter motor, starter solenoid/relay, battery, neutral safety switch, ignition control switch, and connecting wires and cables.

CRT - Cathode ray tube.

Deep cycling - The full discharge and then the full recharge of a battery.

Delta wound - A type of stator winding where all three coils are connected in a triangle shape. Named for the triangle-shape Greek capital letter.

Digital - A method of display that uses numbers instead of a needle or similar device.

Dimmer switch - An electrical switch used to direct the current to either bright or dim headlight filaments.

Diode - An electrical one-way check valve made from combining a P-type material and an N-type material.

Diode trio - A group of three diodes grouped together with one output used to put out the charge indicator lamp and provide current for the field from the stator windings on many alternators.

Direct current - Electric current that flows in one direction.

Distributor - Electromechanical unit used to help create and distribute the high voltage necessary for spark ignition.

DPDT switch - Double-pole, double-throw switch.

Duty cycle - Refers to the percentage of on-time of the signal during one complete cycle.

Earth ground - The most grounded ground. A ground is commonly used as a return current path for an electrical circuit.

EEPROM - Electronically erasable programmable read-only memory.

EFI - Electronic fuel injection.

Electricity - The movement of free electrons from one atom to another.

Electrolyte - Any substance which, in solution, is separated into ions and is made capable of conducting an electric current. The acid solution of a lead-acid battery.

Electromagnetic gauges - A type of dash instrument gauge that uses small electromagnetic coils for the needle movement of the gauge.

Electromagnetic induction - First discovered in 1831 by Michael Faraday, it is the generation of a current in a conductor that is moved through a magnetic field.

Electromagnetism - A magnetic field created by current flow through a conductor.

Electromotive force - The force (pressure) that can move electrons through a conductor.

Electron - A negative-charged particle: 1/1800 the mass of a proton.

Electron theory - The theory that electricity flows from negative (-) to positive (+).

Electronic circuit breaker - See PTC.

EMF - Electromotive force.

Emitter - The name of one section of a transistor. The arrow used on a symbol for a transistor is on the emitter and the arrow points toward the negative section of the transistor.

EPROM - Erasable programmable read-only memory.

Farad - A unit of capacitance named for Michael Faraday (1791–1867), an English physicist. A farad is the capacity to store 1 coulomb of electrons at 1 volt of potential difference.

Feedback - The reverse flow of electrical current through a circuit or electrical unit that should not normally be operating. This feedback current (reverse-bias current flow) is most often caused by a poor ground connection for the same normally operating circuit.

Fiber optics - The transmission of light through special plastic that keeps the light rays parallel even if the plastic is tied in a knot.

Field coils - Coils of wire wound around metal pole shoes to form the electromagnetic field inside an electric motor.

Filament - The light-producing wire inside a light bulb.

FM - Frequency modulation.

Forward bias - Current flow in normal direction.

Frequency - The number of cycles per second, measured in hertz.

Full fielding - The method of supplying full battery voltage to the magnetic field of a generator as part of the troubleshooting procedure for the charging system.

Fuse - An electrical safety unit constructed of a fine tin conductor that will melt and open the electrical circuit if excessive current flows through the fuse.

Fusible link - A type of fuse that will melt and open the protected circuit in the event of a short circuit, which could cause excessive current flow through the fusible link. Most fusible links are actually wires four gauge sizes smaller than the wire of the circuits being protected.

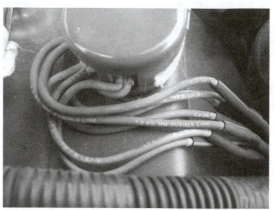

Gassing - The release of hydrogen and oxygen gas from the plates of a battery during charging or discharging.

Gauge - Wire sizes as assigned by the American Wire Gauge system; the smaller the gauge number, the larger the wire.

Gauss - A unit of magnetic induction or magnetic intensity named for Karl Friedrich Gauss (1777–1855), a German mathematician.

Generator - A device that converts mechanical energy into electrical energy.

Grid - The lead-alloy framework (support) for the active materials of an automotive battery.

Ground - The lowest possible voltage potential in a circuit. In electrical terms, a ground is the desirable return circuit path. Ground can also be undesirable and provide a shortcut path for a defective electrical circuit.

Growler - Electrical tester designed to test starters and starter armatures.

Hall effect sensor - A type of electromagnetic sensor used in electronic ignition and other systems. Named for Edward H. Hall, who discovered the Hall effect in 1879.

Hazard flasher - Emergency warning flashers; lights at all four corners of the vehicle flash on and off.

Heat sink - Usually, a metallic finned unit used to keep electronic components cool.

Hold-in winding - One of two electromagnetic windings inside a solenoid; used to hold the movable core into the solenoid.

Hybrid - Something (such as a battery) made from at least two different elements.

Hydrometer - An instrument used to measure the specific gravity of a liquid. A battery hydrometer is calibrated to read the expected specific gravity of battery electrolyte.

Inductive reactance - An opposing current created in a conductor whenever there is a charging current flow in a conductor.

Insulator - A material that does not readily conduct electricity and heat. A nonmetal material that contains more than four electrons in its atom's outer shell.

Ion - An atom with an excess or deficiency of electrons forming either a negative or a positive charged particle.

IVR - Instrument voltage regulator. An IVR is used to maintain constant voltage to thermoelectric gauges to maintain accuracy.

Joule - A unit of electrical energy. One joule equals 1 watt $\times$ 1 second (1 V $\times$ 1 A $\times$ 1 s).

Jumper cables - Heavy-gauge (4 to 00) electrical cables with large clamps, used to connect a vehicle that has a discharged battery to a vehicle that has a good battery.

Kilo - Means 1000; abbreviated k or K.

Kirchhoff's current law - A law that states "The current flowing into any junction of an electrical circuit is equal to the current flowing out of that junction."

Kirchhoff's voltage law - A law about electrical circuits that states: "The voltage around any closed circuit is equal to the sum (total) of the voltage drops."

LCD - Liquid-crystal display.

Lead peroxide - The positive plate of an automotive-style battery; the chemical symbol is PbO_2.

Lead sulfate - Both battery plates become lead sulfate when the battery is discharged. The chemical symbol for lead sulfate is $PbSO_4$.

LED - Light-emitting diode.

Lumbar - The lower section of the back.

Magnequench - A magnetic alloy made from neodymium, iron, and boron.

Module - A group of electronic components functioning as a component of a larger system.

Mutual induction - The generation of an electric current due to a changing magnetic field of an adjacent coil.

Neutrons - A neutral-charged particle; one of the basic particles of the nucleus of an atom.

NTC - Negative temperature coefficient. Usually used in reference to a temperature sensor (coolant or air temperature). As the temperature increases, the resistance of the sensor decreases.
Ohm The unit of electrical resistance. Named for Georg Simon Ohm (1787–1854).

Ohmmeter - An electrical test instrument used to measure ohms (unit of electrical resistance). An ohmmeter uses an internal battery for power and must never be used when current is flowing through a circuit or component.

Ohm's law - An electrical law that states: "It requires 1 volt to push 1 ampere through 1 *ohm* of resistance."

Ω Omega - The last letter of the Greek alphabet; a symbol for ohm, the unit for electrical resistance.

Open circuit - An open circuit is any circuit that is not complete and in which no current flows.

Oscilloscope - A visual display of electrical waves on a fluorescent screen or cathode ray tube.

Partitions - Separations between the cells of a battery. Partitions are made of the same material as that of the outside case of the battery.

Pasting - The process of applying active battery materials onto the grid framework of each plate.

Peak inverse voltage (PIV) - The rating of resistance to reverse-bias voltage. Also called peak reverse voltage (PRV).

Permalloy - A permanent-magnet alloy of nickel and iron.

Photoelectric principle - The production of electricity created by light striking certain sensitive materials, such as selenium or cesium.

Piezoelectric principle - The principle by which certain crystals become electrically charged when pressure is applied.

Pinion gear - A small gear on the end of the starter drive which rotates the engine flywheel ring gear for starting.

PM motor - A permanent-magnet electric motor.

Polarity - The condition of being positive or negative in relation to a magnetic pole.

Porous lead - Lead with many small holes to make a surface porous for use in battery negative plates; the chemical symbol for lead is Pb.

Power side - The wires leading from the power source (battery) to the resistance (load) of a circuit.

Proton - A positive-charged particle; one of the basic particles of the nucleus of an atom.

PRV - See *peak inverse voltage.*

PTC - Positive temperature coefficient. Normally used in reference to a conductor or electronic circuit breaker. As the temperature increases, the electrical resistance also increases.

P-type material - Silicon or germanium doped with boron or indium.

Pull-in windings - One of two electromagnetic windings inside a solenoid used to move a movable core.

Pulse generators - An electromagnetic unit that generates a   voltage signal used to trigger the ignition control module that controls (turns on and off) the primary ignition current of an electronic ignition system.

Pulse train - DC voltage that turns on and off in a series of pulses.

Pulse width modulation (PWM) - The control of a device by varying the amount of on-time current flowing through the device.

Radio choke - A small coil of wire installed in the power lead leading to a pulsing unit such as an IVR to prevent radio interference.

Rectifier - An electronic device that converts alternating current into direct current.

Rectifier bridge - A group of six diodes, three positive (+) and three negative (-) commonly used in alternators.

Relay - An electromagnetic switch that uses a movable arm.

Reluctance - The resistance to the movement of magnetic lines of force.

Reserve capacity - The number of minutes a battery can produce 25 A and still maintain a battery voltage of 1.75 V per cell (10.5 V for a 12-V battery).

Residual magnetism - Magnetism remaining after the magnetizing force is removed.

Resistance - The opposition to current flow.

Reverse bias - Current flow in the opposite direction from normal.

Rheostat - An adjustable variable resistor.

ROM - Read-only memory.

RPM - Revolutions per minute.

RTV - Room-temperature vulcanization.

Sediment chamber - A space below the cell plates of some batteries to permit the accumulation of sediment deposits flaking from the battery plates. Use of a sediment chamber keeps the sediment from shorting the battery plates.

Self-induction - The generation of an electric current in the wires of a coil created when the current is first connected or disconnected.

Semiconductor - A material that is neither a conductor nor an insulator; has exactly four electrons in the atom's outer shell.

Separators - In a battery, nonconducting porous, thin materials used to separate positive and negative plates.

Series-parallel circuit - Any type of circuit containing resistances in both series and parallel in one circuit.

Series wound - In a starter motor, the field coils and the armature are wired in series. All current flows through the field coils, through the hot brushes, through the armature, then to the ground through the ground brushes.

Servo unit - A vacuum-operated unit that attaches to the throttle linkage to move the throttle on a cruise control system.

Shelf life - The length of time that something can remain on a storage shelf and not be reduced in performance level from that of a newly manufactured product.

Short circuit - A circuit in which current flows, but bypasses some or all of the resistance in the circuit. A connection that results in a copper-to-copper connection.

Short to ground - A short circuit in which the current bypasses some or all of the resistance of the circuit and flows to ground. Since ground is usually steel in automotive electricity, a short-to-ground (grounded) is a copper-to-steel connection.

Shunt - A device used to divert or bypass part of the current from the main circuit.

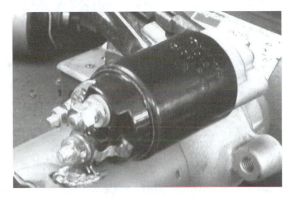

Solenoid - An electromagnetic switch that uses a movable core.

Specific gravity - The ratio of the weight of a given volume of a liquid divided by the weight of an equal volume of water.

Sponge lead - Lead with many small holes used to make a surface porous or sponge-like for use in battery negative plates; the chemical symbol for lead is Pb.

Starter drive - A term used to describe the starter motor drive pinion gear with overrunning clutch.

State of charge - The degree or the amount that a battery is charged. A fully charged battery would be 100% charged.

Stator - A name for three interconnected windings inside an alternator. A rotating rotor provides a moving magnetic field and induces a current in the windings of the stator.

Tell-tale light - Dash warning light.

Thermistor - A resistor that changes resistance with temperature. A positive-coefficient thermistor has increased resistance with an increase in temperature. A negative-coefficient thermistor has increased resistance with a decrease in temperature.

Thermoelectric meters - A type of dash instrument that uses heat created by current flow through the gauge to deflect the indicator needle.

Thermoelectric principle - The production of current flow created by heating the connection of two dissimilar metals.

Torque - A twisting force which may or may not result in motion.

Trade number - The number stamped on an automotive light bulb. All bulbs of the same trade number have the same candlepower and wattage, regardless of the manufacturer of the bulb.

Transducer - An electrical and mechanical speed-sensing and control unit used on cruise control systems.

Transistor - A semiconductor device that can operate as an amplifier or an electrical switch.

Volt - The unit of electrical pressure; named for Alessandro Volta (1745–1827).

Voltage regulator - An electronic or mechanical unit that controls the output voltage of an electrical generator or alternator by controlling the field current of the generator.

Voltmeter - An electrical test instrument used to measure volts (unit of electrical potential). A voltmeter is connected in parallel with the unit or circuit being tested.

VTF - Vacuum-tube fluorescent.

Watt - An electrical unit of power (1/746 hp); watts equal current (amperes) × voltage. Named after James Watt, a Scottish inventor.

Wye wound - A type of stator winding in which all three coils are connected to a common center connection. Called a wye because the connections look like the letter Y.

Zener diode - A specially constructed (heavily doped) diode designed to operate with a reverse-bias current after a certain voltage has been reached. Named for Clarence Melvin Zener.

A6 Spanish-Language Glossary

Alternator – alternador. Generador de corriente eléctrica que produce corriente alterna pero que se rectifica a la corriente directa por medio de diodos. También se llama *AC generator (generador de corriente alterna)*.

AM (amplitude modulation) – amplitud modulada.

Ammeter – amperímetro/amperómetro/ametro. Instrumento eléctrico que sirve para medir amperios (unidad de la intensidad de corriente eléctrica).

Ampere – amperio. Unidad que mide la intensidad de corriente eléctrica. Llamada en honor de Andre Ampere (1775–1836).

Ampere turns - amperio-vueltas - Unidad de medid de la fuerza magnética de un campo eléctrico.

Analog – análogo. Clase de instrumento del tablero de dirección/salpicadero que indica valores por medio del movimiento de un aguja o aparato parecido. Una señal análoga es continua y variable.

Anode – ánodo. Electrodo positivo hacia el cual fluyen los electrones.

Antimony – antimonio. Metal que se añade a la placa una batería híbrida o libre de mantenimiento y que sirve para endurecerla.

Armature – armadura. Unidad que gira dentro de un generador de DC o arrancador que consta de bobinas de alambre aislante enrolladas sobre un núcleo de hierro dulce.

Atom – átomo. La unidad más pequeña de materia que tiene características propias.

AWG (American wire gauge system) – sistema americano de calibrador de alambre.

Backlight – luz trasera. Luz que ilumina el despliegue del instrumento de prueba por detrás del VCL o desde la ventana trasera de un automóvil.

Bakelite – Marca de la Union Carbide Company para plástico de resina fenolformaldehida.

Base – base. Parte de un transistor que controla el flujo de corriente a través del transistor.

Battery – batería. Aparato químico que produce voltaje por medio de dos metales distintos sumergidos en un electrolito.

Bendix drive – mecanismo de arranque Bendix. Mecanismo inercial de arranque; a partir de los 1960 no se ha utilizado para automóviles.

Bias - polarización - En términos eléctricos, el voltaje aplicado a un dispositivo o componente de un circuito para establecer un punto de referencia para su operación.

Blower-motor – motor del ventilador. Motor eléctrico con un abanico que circula el aire dentro del automóvil para calentarlo, enfriarlo y descongelarlo.

BNC connector – conector BNC. Conector coaxial que normalmente se usa en los osciloscopios. Llamado en honor de su inventor, Baby Neil Councilman.

Brushes – brochas/escobillas. Conductor de cobre o carbono que se utiliza para trasladar corriente eléctrica a o de una parte eléctrica que gira, como la que se encuentra en un motor o generador eléctrico.

Burn in - calentamiento - El proceso de operar un dispositivo electrónico por un periodo de tiempo que puede ir de unas horas a varios días.

Calcium – calcio. Elemento metálico que se añade a los armazones de una batería libre de mantenimiento para fortalecerlos.

Candlepower – potencia lumínica. Medida de la cantidad de luz que produce una bombilla.

Capacitance – capacidad. Mide la carga que puede almacenar un capacitor/condensador dado la diferencia de potencial de voltaje. Se mide en faradios o en incrementos más pequeños, como microfaradios.

Capacitor – capacitor. También se llama *condensor (condensador)*. Unidad eléctrica que puede trasladar corriente alterna pero que a la vez bloquear corriente directa; se usa en circuitos eléctricos para controlar las fluctuaciones de voltaje.

Carbon pile – pila de carbono. Instrumento eléctrico de prueba que se usa para proporcionar una carga eléctrica para probar baterías y el circuito de carga.

Cathode – cátodo. El electrodo negativo.

Cell – pila. Grupo de platos negativos y positivos capaz de producir 2.1 voltios.

CEMF (counterelectromotive force) – fuerza contrelectromotriz, contratensión o contravoltaje.

Charging circuit – circuito de carga. Componentes eléctricos y conexiones que se necesitan para mantener la carga total de una batería.

Chassis ground – tierra de chasis. En términos eléctricos, una tierra es el camino deseable para el circuito de retorno.

Circuit – circuito. Un circuito es el camino de los electrones: fluyen de un fuente de poder, a través de una resistencia y vuelven a la fuente de poder.

Circuit breaker – fusible interruptor de circuito. Unidad mecánica que abre un circuito eléctrico a caso de flujo de corriente en exceso.

Cold cranking amperes (CCA) – amperaje de arranque en frío. Valuación de la habilidad de una batería de producir voltaje en tiempo frío.

Collector – colector. Nombre de una parte de un transistor.

Commutator – conmutador. Los segmentos de cobre de armadura de un arrancador o generador de corriente directa.

Composite headlights – faros compósitos. Clase de faro que utiliza una lámpara distinta y reemplazable.

Compound wound - bobinado compuesto - Un tipo de motor eléctrico en el que varias bobinas están conectadas en serie y otras en paralelo con la armadura.

Conductor – conductor. Material que conduce electricidad y calor. Un metal que tiene menos que cuatro electrones en el nivel más alejado del núcleo.

Conventional theory – teoría convencional. Teoriza que electricidad fluye de positivo (+) a negativo (–).

Courtesy light – luz de entrada. Describe todas la luces interiores.

Cranking circuit – circuito de mando. Componentes eléctricos y conexiones que son necesarios para arrancar el motor.

CRT (cathode ray tube) – Tubo de rayos catódicos.

Deep cycling – ciclado/ciclaje completo. Descarga completa de una batería seguida de recarga completa.

Delta wound – enrollo delta. Manera de enrollar el reactor/stator en la cual las tres bobinas se conectan en forma de triángulo.

Digital – digital. Método de despliegue que utilza números en vez de una aguja o aparto parecido.

Dimmer switch – conmutador reductor de intensidad de luz. Conmutador eléctrico que se usa para dirigir la corriente a los filamentos del faro de o alta o baja intensidad.

Diode – diodo. Aparato eléctrico que permite que la corriente fluya en una sola dirección.

Diode trio – trio de diodos. Tres diodos conjuntos con una capacidad que se usa para apagar la lámpara indicadora de carga y proveer corriente para el campo de los enrollos de reactores en muchos alternadores.

Direct current (DC) – corriente directa. Flujo constante de corriente eléctrica que fluye en una sola dirección.

Distributor – distribuidor. Mecanismo electromecánico que se usa para crear y distribuir el voltaje alto necesario para el encendido de chispa.

DPDT (double-pole, double-throw) switch – conmutador bipolar de dos posiciones. Dos circuitos, dos posiciones.

Duty cycle – ciclo de duración. Porcentaje del período de un motor que el motor trabaja o reposa.

Earth ground - toma de tierra - Conexión maestra de tierra. Esta conexión se usa normalmente como camino de retorno de la corriente eléctrica en un circuito.

EEPROM (eletronically erasable programmable read-only memory) – memoria de acceso aleatorio programable y borrable electrónicamente.

EFI (electronic fuel injection) – inyección de combustible electrónica.

Electricity – electricidad. Movimiento de electrones libres de un átomo a otro.

Electrolyte – electrolito. Sustancia que, en solución, se separa en iones y se hace capaz de conducir una corriente eléctrica; la solución ácida de una batería de ácido-plomo.

Electromagnetic gauges – indicadores electromagnéticos. Tipo de instrumento del pescante/tablero que utiliza carretes electromagnéticos pequeños.

Electromagnetic induction – inducción electromagnética. Generación de corriente en un conductor que pasa por un campo magnético. En 1831 Michael Faraday descubrió la inducción electromagnético.

Electromagnetism – electromagnetismo. Campo magnético creado por flujo de corriente por un conductor.

Electromotive force (EMF) – fuerza electromotriz. Fuerza (presión) que puede mover electrones por un conductor.

Electron – electrón. Partícula que lleva carga negativa y que tiene 1/1.800 la masa de un protón.

Electron theory – teoría de electrones. Teoría que dice que electricidad fluye desde negativo (–) a positivo (+).

Electronic circuit breaker – *Véase* PTC.

EMF (electromotive force) – fuerza electromotriz.

Emitter – emisora. Nombre de una parte de un transistor. La flecha que se usa en un símbolo para un transistor se encuentra en la emisora e indica la parte negativa del transistor.

EPROM (erasable programmable read-only memory) – memoria de sólo lectura borrable y programable.

Farad – faradio. Unidad de capacidad. Llamado en honor de Michael Faraday (1791–1867), físico inglés. Un faradio es la capacidad de almacenar 1 coulomb de electrones a 1 voltio de diferencia de potencial.

Feedback – retroalimentación. Flujo al revés de la corriente eléctrica por un circuito o unidad eléctrica que normalmente no debe estar funcionando. Esta corriente retroalimentación (flujo de corriente de retorno) muchas veces se atribuye a un contacto a tierra malo para el mismo circuito que normalmente funciona.

Fiber optics – transimisión por fibra óptica. Transmisión de luz por medio de un plástico especial que mantiene los rayos paralelos aún cuando el plástico se anuda.

Field coils – bobinas de inducción. Bobinas o alambre enrollado en superficies polares de metal para crear un campo magnético dentro de un motor eléctrico.

Filament – filamento. Alambre dentro de una bombilla que produce luz.

FM (frequency modulation) – modulación de frequencia.

Forward bias – corriente de diseño. Flujo de corriente en la dirección normal.

Frequency – frequencia. Número de veces una onda se repite en un segundo, que se mide en Hertz (Hz), en una banda.

Full fielding – exitar el campo al máximo. Método de proveer voltaje al máximo al campo magnético de un generador como parte del procedimiento de la búsqueda de averías para el sistema de carga.

Fuse – fusible. Unidad de seguirdad eléctrica que se construye de un conductor de hojalata fina que se derrite y abre el circuito acaso de un flujo de corriente excesivo.

Fusible link – alambre fusible. Fusible que se derrite y abre el circuito protegido en caso de que haya un circuito corto, lo que puede resultar en el flujo de corriente excesivo por el alambre fusible. La mayoría de los alambres fusibles de hecho son alambres cuyas entrevías son cuarto tamaños más pequeños que el alambre de los circuitos que protegen.

Gassing – proceso de gaseado. Liberación de hidrógeno y oxígeno de los platos de una batería durante cargar o descargar.

Gauge – calibrador. Calibres de alambre asignados por el sistema americano del calibrador de alambre; lo más pequeño el número del calibrador, lo más grande el alambre.

Gauss – gauss. Unidad de inducción o intensidad magnética llamada en honor de Karl Friedrich Gauss (1777–1855), un matemático alemán.

Generator – generador. Artefacto que convierte la energía mecánica en la energía eléctrica.

Grid – cuadrículada/la placa de batería. Armazón (apoyo) de aleación de plomo para las materias activas de una batería automotora.

Ground – tierra. Potencial posible más bajo del voltaje en un circuito. En términos eléctricos, tierra es el sendero deseable de circuito de regreso. Tierra puede ser también indeseable y puede proporcionar un sendero del atajo para un circuito eléctrico defectuoso.

Growler – probador de inducidos. Probador eléctrico diseñado para probar el arrancador y las armaduras del generador de DC.

Hall effect sensor - sensor de efecto Hall - Un tipo de sensor electromagnético usado en sistemas de arranque electrónicos. Llamado así por Edward H. Hall, quien descubrió el efecto que lleva su nombre en 1879.

Hazard flashers – luces de advertencia de peligro. Luces o lámparas que advierten de una emergencia; las luces en los cuatro rincones del vehículo que destellan.

Heat sink – absorbente de calor. Generalmente, una unidad de metal con planos de derive que se usa para mantener frescos los componentes electrónicos.

Hold-in winding – bobinado de sujección. Uno de dos embobinados electromagnéticos dentro de un solenoide; se usa para fijar el núcleo movible del solenoide.

Hybrid – híbrido. Algo (tal como una batería) que se hace de más que un elemento.

Hydrometer – aerómetro. Instrumento que se usa para medir la gravedad específica de un líquido. Un aerómetro de la batería se calibra para medir la gravedad específica esperada de electrólito de batería.

Inductive reactance – reactancia inductiva. Corriente opuesta creada en el conductor cuando hay un flujo de corriente cargadora en el conductor.

Insulator – aislador. Materia que no es buen conductor de electricidad y calor. Una materia no metal que tiene más de cuatro electrones en el nivel exterior del átomo.

Ion – ion. Átomo con un exceso o una deficiencia de electrones que forma una partícula negativamente o positivamente cargada.

IVR (instrument voltage regulator) – regulador del voltaje del instrumento.

Joule - julio - Una unidad de energía eléctrica. Un julio equivale a 1 vatio x 1 segundo (1 Voltio x 1 Amperio x 1 segundo).

Jumper cables – cables para paso de corriente. Cables eléctricos pesados (4 a 00) con abrazaderas grandes que se usan para conectar un vehículo que tiene una batería descargada a otro que tiene una batería buena.

Kilo – kilo. 1.000; se abrevia «k» o «K».

Kirchhoff's current law - ley de Kirchhoff de la corriente eléctrica - Ley sobre circuitos eléctricos que dice que "la corriente eléctrica que llega a cualquier punto de un circuito eléctrico es igual que la corriente que sale de dicho punto."

Kirchhoff's voltage law - **Ley de Kirchhoff del voltaje eléctrico** - Ley sobre circuitos eléctricos que dice que "el voltaje en un circuito cerrado es igual a la suma de todas las voltajes."

LCD (liquid crystal display) – VCL. Visualizador de cristal líquido.

Lead peroxide – peróxido de plomo. El plato positivo de una batería del estilo automotriz. El símbolo químico es PbO_2.

Lead sulfate – sulfato de plomo. Ambos platos de batería se hacen sulfato de plomo cuando la batería se descarga. El símbolo químico para el sulfato de plomo es $PbSO_4$.

LED (light-emitting diode) – diodo luminoso.

Lumbar – lumbar. Parte más baja de la espalda.

Magnequench - Una aleación magnética de neodimio, hierro y boro.

Module – módulo. Grupo de componentes electrónicos que funcionan como un sólo componente de un sistema más grande.

Mutual induction – inducción mutua. Generación de una corriente eléctrica debido a un campo magnético cambiante de un rollo adyacente.

Neutrons – neutrones. Partícula con carga neutral; uno de las partículas básicas del núcleo de un átomo.

NTC (negative temperature coefficient) – coeficiente de temperatura negativo. Generalmente que se usa en referencia a un sensor de la temperatura (líquido refrigerante o temperatura aérea). Mientras que la temperatura se aumenta, la resistencia del sensor se disminuye.

Ohm – ohmio. Unidad de la resistencia eléctrica; llamada en honor de Georg Simon Ohm (1787–1854).

Ohmmeter – ohmiómetro. Instrumento de prueba eléctrico que se usa para medir los ohmios (unidad de la resistencia eléctrica).

Ohm's law – ley de Ohm. Ley eléctrica que dice que se necesita 1 voltio para mover 1 amperio por 1 ohmio de resistencia.

Ω (omega) – omega. Última letra del alfabeto griego; símbolo para el ohmio (Ω), la unidad de resistencia eléctrica.

Open circuit – circuito abierto. Circuito que no es completo y por lo cual no corriente fluye.

Oscilloscope – osciloscopio. Despliegue visual de ondas eléctricas en una pantalla fluorescente o en un tubo de rayos catódicos.

Partitions – divisiones. Separaciones entre las células de una batería. Las divisiones se hacen de la misma materia que el caso exterior de la batería.

Pasting – pegar. Proceso de aplicar las materias activas de batería a la armazón cuadrículada de cada plato.

Peak inverse voltage (PIV) - voltaje punta inverso - La clasificación de la resistencia a un voltaje de polarización inversa. También llamado máximo voltaje inverso (PRV).

Permalloy – Aleación magnética permanente de níquel e hierro.

Photoelectric principle – principio fotoeléctrico. Producción de electricidad creada por la luz al atacar ciertas materias sensibles, tal como selenio o cesio.

Piezoelectric principle – principio piezoeléctrico. Principio por lo cuál ciertos cristales llegan a ser cargados eléctricamente cuando se aplica presión.

Pinion gear – piñón satélite. Engranaje pequeño en el extremo del mecanismo de arranque que gira el engranaje anualar del volante del motor para arrancar.

PM (permanent magnet) motor – motor PM. Motor eléctrico de imán permanente.

Polarity – polaridad. Condición de ser positivo o negativo con relación a un polo magnético.

Power side - circuito de carga - La conexión eléctrica que va de la fuente de alimentación (batería) a la resistencia (carga) de un circuito.

Proton – protón. Partícula positivamente cargada; una de las partículas básicas del núcleo de un átomo.

PRV - *Ver* voltaje punta inverso.

PTC – *Véase* positive temperature coefficient.

P-type material – material del tipo P. Silicio o germanio dopado con boro o indio.

Pull-in windings – bobina de tracción. Una de dos bobinas electromagnéticas dentro de un solenoide que se usa para mover un núcleo movible.

Pulse generators – generadores de pulso. Unidad electromagnética que genera una señal de voltaje que se usa para provocar el mando del encendido que conecta y desconecta la corriente primaria del encendido de un sistema de encendido electrónico.

Pulse train – tren de pulso. Voltaje de DC que se conecta y se desconecta en una serie de pulsos.

Pulse width modulation (PWM) – modulación de la anchura de pulso. Operación de un artefacto por una señal digital binaria que se controla según la duración de tiempo que el artefacto está conectado y desconectado.

Radio choke - obstructor de interferencias - Un pequeño bobinado instalado en la toma de corriente que elimina interferencias de señales de radio.

Rectifier – convertidor. Artefacto electrónico que convierte corriente alterna en corriente directa.

Rectifier bridge – puente rectificador. Grupo de seis diodos, tres positivos (+) y tres negativo (–) que se usa comúnmente en alternadores.

Relay – relevador. Interruptor electromagnético que usa un brazo movible.

Reluctance – reluctancia. Resistencia al movimiento de líneas magnéticas de la fuerza.

Residual magnetism – magnetismo residual. Magnetismo que se queda después que la fuerza magnetizante se quita.

Resistance – resistencia. Oposición al flujo de corriente que se mide en ohmios.

Reverse bias – corriente de retorno. Flujo de corriente en la dirección opuesta del flujo normal.

Rheostat – reóstato. Resistor variable de dos terminales.

ROM (read-only memory) – memoria de sólo lectura.

RPM (revolutions per minute) – velocidad del motor que se expresa en revoluciones del cingüeñal por minuto.

RTV (room-temperature vulcanization) – vulcanización de temperatura ambiente.

Sediment chamber - cámara de sedimentos - Espacio situado debajo de lor bornes de algunas pilas o baterías para permitir la acumulación de sedimentos que se desprenden de dichos bornes. El uso de esta cámara elimina la posibilidad de un cortocircuito en la batería.

Self-induction – autoinducción. Generación de una corriente eléctrica en los alambres de una bobina que se crea cuando la corriente primero se conecta o desconecta.

Semiconductor – semiconductor. Materia que es ni conductor ni aislador y que tiene exactamente cuatro electrones en el nivel exterior de átomo.

Series-parallel circuit - circuito en series-paralelo - Cualquier tipo de circuito eléctrico que contiene resistencias tanto en serie como en paralelo en un solo circuito.

Series wound – arrollado en serie. En un motor de arranque, las bobinas inductoras y la armadura se alambran en la serie. Toda corriente fluye por las bobinas inductoras, las escobillas de tensión, la armadura y entonces por las escobillas de tierra al suelo.

Servo unit – unidad de servo. Unidad operada de vacío en un sistema de control de crucero que conecta a las articulaciones de acelerador para mover el acelerador.

Shelf life – tiempo de durabilidad antes de la venta. Plazo de tiempo que algo puede permanecer en un estante de almacenamiento sin que el nivel de desempeño se reduzca del desempeño de un producto que se acaba de fabricar.

Short circuit – circuito corto. Circuito en que la corriente fluye pero evita un poco de o toda la resistencia en el circuito; una conexión que tiene como resultado una conexión «cobre a cobre».

Short to ground – corto a tierra. Circuito corto por lo cual la corriente fluye pero evita algo de o toda la resistencia en el circuito y fluye a tierra. Porque el suelo es generalmente acero en la electricidad automotriz, un corto a tierra (puesto a tierra) es una conexión «cobre a acero».

Shunt – derivación. Artefacto que se usa para desviar o evitar parte de la corriente del circuito principal.

Solenoid – solenoide. Interruptor electromagnético que usa un núcleo movible.

Specific gravity – peso específico. Ratio del peso del volumen de un líquido dado dividido entre el peso del mismo volumen de agua.

Sponge lead – esponja de plomo. Plomo hecho con muchos hoyos pequeños para que su superficie sea porosa o como una esponja para uso en platos negativos de batería; el símbolo químico para el plomo es *Pb*.

Starter drive – transmisión de motor de arranque. Término que se usa para describir el piñón satélite de propulsión del motor de arranque con acoplamiento libre.

State of charge – estado de carga. Grado o cantidad que una batería está cargada. Una batería completamente cargada sería 100 por ciento cargada.

Stator – estator. Nombre para tres bobinados interconectados dentro de un alternador. Un inducido giratorio provee un campo magnético móvil e induce una corriente en los bobinados del estator.

Tell-tale light – lámpara de aviso. Lámpara de advertir del tablero (a veces se llama *idiot light (luz de idiota).*

Thermistor – termistor. Resistor que varía su resistencia según la temperatura. Un termistor de coeficiente positivo aumenta la resistencia cuando se aumenta la temperatura. Un termistor de coeficiente negativo aumenta la resistencia con una disminución de temperatura.

Thermoelectric meters - medidor termoeléctrico - Un tipo de instrumentación que utiliza el calor creado por el paso de una corriente eléctrica por un calibre para mover la aguja indicadora.

Thermoelectric principle – principio termoeléctrico. Producción del flujo de corriente creado calentando la conexión de dos metales distintos.

Torque – torque/torsión. Fuerza que tuerce que se mide en libras pies (lb-ft) o Newton–metros (N–m), que pueda resultar en movimiento.

Trade number – número de comercio. Número estampado en un bombillo automotriz. Cada bombillo del mismo número de comercio tiene la misma potencia lumínicia y vatiaje, a pesar del fabricante de la bombilla.

Transducer – transductor. Unidad de control eléctrica y mecánica que presiente la velocidad que se usa en sistemas de control de crucero.

Transistor – transistor. Artefacto semiconductor que puede operar como amplificador o interruptor eléctrico.

Volt – voltio. Unidad para la cantidad de presión eléctrica; llamado en honor de Alessandro Volta (1745–1827).

Voltage regulator – regulador de voltaje. Unidad electrónica o mecánica que controla la tensión final de un generador o alternador por controlar la corriente de campo del generador.

Voltmeter – voltímetro. Instrumento eléctrico de la prueba que se usa para medir los voltios (la unidad de la presión eléctrica). El voltímetro se conecta en paralelo con la unidad o el circuito que se está probando.

VTF (vacuum-tube fluorescent) – tubo fluorescente de vacío.

Watt – vatio. Unidad eléctrica de poder; un vatio (1/746 hp) iguala el voltaje por la corriente. Llamado en honor de James Watt, inventor escocés.

Wye wound – enrollado en forma de «Y». Tipo de bobinado de estator en que tres rollos son conectados a una conexión común y central. Se llama *wye(i griega)* porque las conexiones se parecen a la letra «Y».

Zener diode – diodo-Zener. Diode especialmente construido (muy dopado) diseñado para operar con una corriente de corriente de retorno después de que se alcance un cierto voltaje. Llamado en honor de Clarence Melvin Zener.

Index